Problem-Solving Situations

A Teacher's Resource Book

VOLUME 1

WRITTEN AND ILLUSTRATED BY

Joel Greenberg

A GRAPEVINE PUBLICATION

Research Library
AIMS Education Foundation
Fresno, CA 93747-8120

HIEBERT LIBRARY
FRESNO PACIFIC UNIV
FRESNO, CA 93702

Acknowledgments

Elmer's Glue refers to Elmer's Glue-All, the registered trade name of the glue product of Borden, Inc. Kix is the registered trade name of the breakfast cereal product of General Mills, Inc. Morton's refers to the boxed salt product of Morton Salt Co. Pepsi and Pepsi-Cola are registered trademarks of PepsiCo, Inc. Scotch brand adhesive tape is a product of 3M Company.

Cover illustration by Matthew C. Coffin

© 1990, Joel Greenberg. All rights reserved. No portion of this book or its contents, may be reproduced in any form, printed, electronic or mechanical, without written permission from Joel Greenberg and Grapevine Publications, Inc.

Printed in the United States of America
ISBN 0-931011-14-0

First Printing – December, 1990

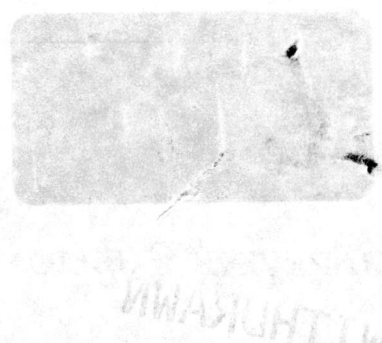

This book is dedicated to Joanne, who walked the walk and talked the talk, and to Elmer's Glue.

Contents

Introduction 8

    WHAT ARE PROBLEM-SOLVING SITUATIONS? 13

    WHO CAN USE THIS BOOK? 15

    HOW TO USE PROBLEM-SOLVING SITUATIONS 17
        I.   Preparation and Planning 18
        II.   Presentation to the Class 22
        III.   Problem Solving in Small Groups 24
        IV.   Evaluation as a Class 28
        V.   After Testing The Prediction: The Next Step 30

    GETTING YOUR ... STUFF TOGETHER 32

The Problem-Solving Situations 34

I. LENGTH, NUMBER AND WEIGHT 34

Section Notes 35
1: The Doodah 36
2: Paper Stack 38
3: Toilet Paper 40
4: The Weight of Water 43
5: Pennies in a Bottle 46
6: Kix Are For Kids 48
7: Wood 50
Notes (Yours) 53

II. SPEED AND DISTANCE 54

Section Notes 55
8: Unicycle Walk 56
9: Driveby 58
10: Twenty-Minute Walk 60
11: Untimed Walk 62
12: Head On 64

III. CIRCUMFERENCE AND AREA 66

Section Notes 67
13: Garbage 68
14: Around and Through 70
15: Boxed Wheels 72
16: In and Out 76
Notes (Yours) 79

IV. AREA AND WEIGHT 80

- Section Notes 81
- 17: Two Pieces of Wood 82
- 18: Triangle and Rectangle with Bread 84
- 19: Two for One 86
- 20: Circular Reasoning 87
- 21: Scratchy Snoods 88
- 22: Out of Whack 90
- 23: Planely Shaped 92
- Notes (Yours) 93

V. DENSITY, WEIGHT, AND VOLUME 94

- Section Notes 95
- 24: Doodah #2 96
- 25: Shampoo Bottle 98
- 26: Boxawaddah 100
- 27: Heavy Can 102
- 28: Pepsi Generation 104
- 29: Radically Tubular, Fersure 106
- 30: Tubesoak 108
- Notes (Yours) 109

VI. DENSITY AND IDENTITY 110

- Section Notes 111
- 31: Three Bottles 112
- 32: Prospecting 114
- 33: Hollow Box 116

VII. TRIANGULATION 118

- Section Notes 119
- 34: Hose Tower 120
- 35: Telephone Pole 122

| VIII. | Flotation and Displacement | 124 |

    Section Notes 125
    36: Don't Cry Over Spilled Milk 126
    37: Lucite Rod 128
    38: Balloons 129
    39: End of the Year 132

| IX. | Odds and Ends | 134 |

    Section Notes 135
    40: Looking Down and Out 136
    41: Cuban Missile Base 137
    42: Heavy Water 139
    43: Fire Hose 141
    44: Rain Gutter 142
    45: Puddle 143
    46: Salt Shaker 144
    47: Heavy 145

For Future Thought 146

More Problem-Solving Situations 147

A Precollege Math/Science Curriculum 148

About Grapevine Publications 150

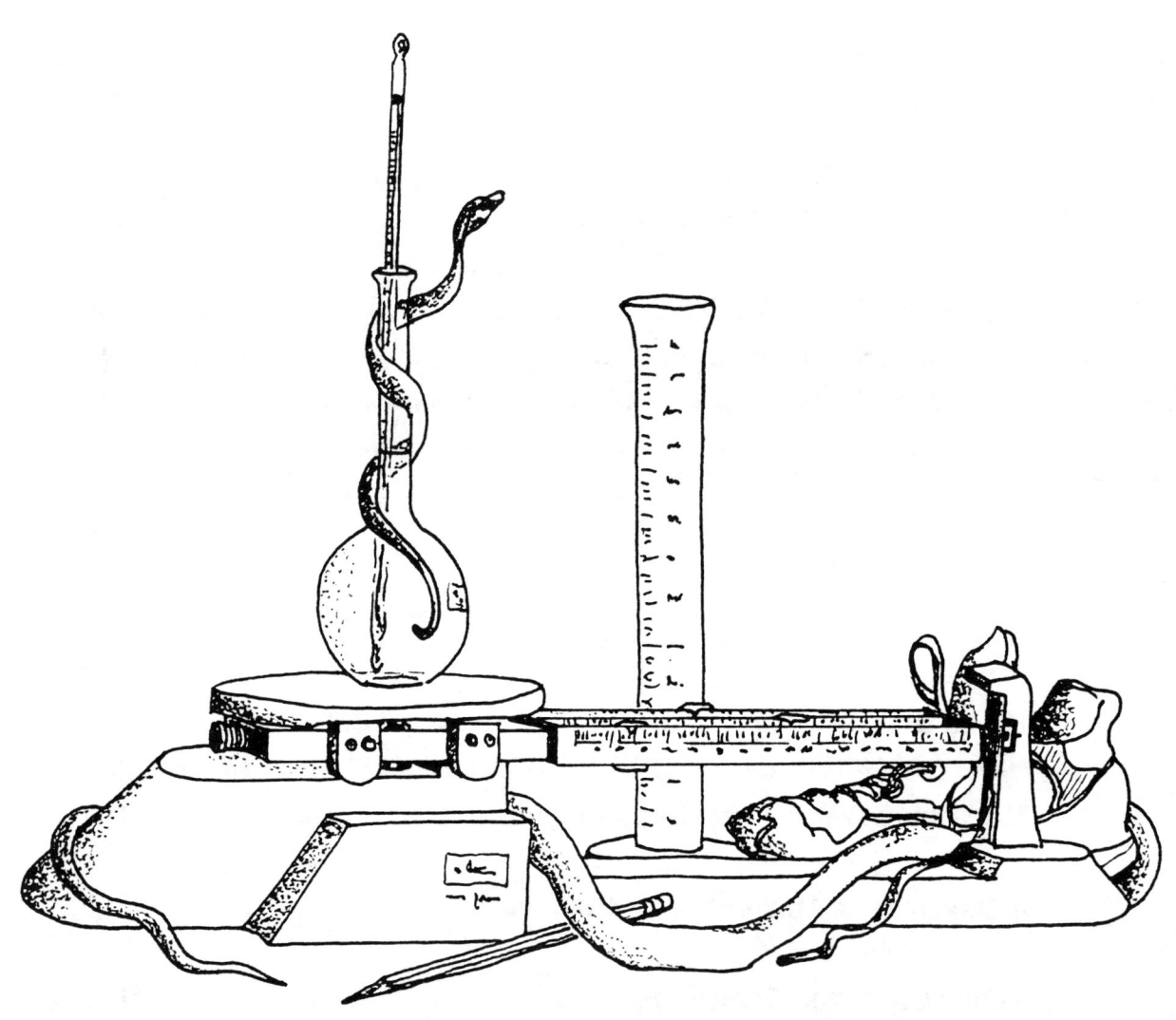

INTRODUCTION

The numbing ineffectiveness of our math and science curricula has been much in the news. The experts have portioned out the blame for the situation to three kinds of problems:

1. Failure to teach what are often called "problem-solving" or critical thinking skills—the skills needed to analyze and attack problems.

2. Failure to teach the "basics"—the facts, theories and operations needed to inform and carry out problem-solving attack strategies.

3. Failure to make the subjects exciting, stimulating and relevant.

In most instances, we have responded by addressing each of these failures separately. The results of this single-track approach have been universally unsatisfactory for teachers, students, and parents. As teachers, we constantly face the dilemma of balancing time spent on the basics against time spent on problem-solving skills. Additionally, we're expected to do this in a stimulating way.

In some schools, we are asked to teach basics. In others, the curriculum is tipped in the opposite direction. Still other programs ask us to concentrate on making science and math fun. Each time we focus on one aspect of the problem, the other two rise up in its place. Whatever the emphasis, the overall situation seems unchanged. Our kids still perform poorly by almost all relevant measures. They rarely seem able to integrate basic skills and facts into effective problem-solving activities.

You can easily understand just how great this difficulty is by observing the large numbers of students (and adults) who have "mastered" science concepts and math skills separately, but are unable to apply them. These people seem to understand a certain chunk of theory and some basic physical concepts. They don't, for example, expect steel balls to float in water, They know that apples fall when dropped from trees. They know that $1.50 is less than $15.00. They seem able to negotiate the day-to-day world competently.

Introduction

In addition, they have learned all of the skills thought necessary to use and apply these basic science and math concepts. They can, for instance, solve pages and pages of problems that require the division of fractions. They know the operation—"flip the second one and multiply across. Nevertheless, they just don't seem able to put the two pieces, skill and theory, together in a useful way. They can learn formulae, procedures and cookbook methods for solving certain types of problems but are only marginally able to recognize which problems they face in real-life situations. They cannot choose when to add, multiply, subtract, or divide.

In short, many apparently well-educated students fail to use (or trust) concepts "learned" in math and science classes. Picture the student who, staring at 20 division problems says, "just show me how to do the first one and I'll do the rest of the page." Or perhaps you're more familiar with the science student who shows you perfectly performed math operations that "prove" a steel ball-bearing will float in water, "because the answer is 7.31g."

A surprising number of adults are similarly limited in their ability to apply basic concepts of the physical world to practical problems. In fact, many teachers (including science and math teachers) have only a "because-it-works" kind of knowledge of even the most fundamental physical properties. They can identify or explain pertinent concepts but cannot use those concepts flexibly or powerfully when confronted with unfamiliar situations requiring interpretation and real understanding.

This situation isn't surprising when we consider the almost uninterrupted parade of texts and curricula that present and organize concepts and their uses separately. Word problems, as afterthoughts or "bonus problems," form but a half-hearted acknowledgment of the necessary linkage between concept, skill, and practical command in science and math. Given such short shrift, these problems are, predictably, nightmares for most students. There isn't a teachers' lounge in the U.S. where you won't hear teachers venting their befuddled frustration with students who "know the material," but can't "do" the word problems at the end of the chapter.

Of course, some students who have better-developed abstracting skills, are enrolled in intensely experimental (lab-oriented) science courses in high school. Poor science and math students, on the other hand, are rarely enrolled in such programs because of deficient skills. The lab activities that they need, it is reasoned, are "beyond their skill profiles."

These unfortunate students typically work with two strikes against them. First, they rarely understand concepts of the physical world adequately. And even when they do, they are unable and unwilling to use those concepts in the proximity of numbers. These students not only know less than others, they are unable to use what they <u>do</u> know. They cannot connect their practical knowledge to the "school stuff" which so bedevils them.

Secondly, these disadvantaged students often lack the abilities to easily learn and memorize processes and procedures that might partially compensate for conceptual deficits. Typically they can't remember whether to move the decimal point to the right or the left. More unfortunate, though, they are unable to make an educated guess based on what the two alternatives might mean in a real-world situation. If they learn one side of the theory/skill configuration, it does nothing to illuminate the other side of the picture. For them, there is no connection between the two. Indeed, they see math operations as "stuff you do" rather than as methods for observing and organizing data.

At best, therefore, many students will learn math skills and science concepts as separate subjects—despite occasional lip service to the contrary. Too often we assume that they cannot benefit from an experimental approach because of skill deficits in math. Remedial teachers can corroborate how many times these students seem to "learn" a scientific or math concept only to "lose" it as soon as they are faced with its application.

The approach most commonly adopted to address this difficulty is endless drill. Occasionally, in "progressive" situations, unsuccessful students are instead asked to observe or perform endless "experiments" which normally possess no quantitative or informed predictive aspect whatsoever. This is the "Golly-Gee" arm of science, and while it's perhaps more stimulating and fun for its victims, this "science" presents the world merely as a place of impenetrable magic and "neat" effects. Solutions boil; bubbles form; bangs happen.

In most science programs, there is no real linkage between the skills needed to observe and organize data, and the concepts needed to interpret and guide the operation. Skill and theory are typically presented as separate aspects of reality, hermetically sealed away from one another. Thus teachers and curriculum consultants, like the students whom they would help, fail to recognize the futility of learning one side of the coin without the other.

What Are Problem-Solving Situations?

Problem-Solving Situations are encounters with real-world problems that require students to make testable predictions. Usually, the predictions require some combination of measurement, observation, estimation, and calculation. The choice and design of problem-solving methodologies is left to the students. The "answer" to the problem is always provided by an actual test of the prediction.

Problem-Solving Situations reinforce the natural links between experience, concept formation, math, and science. The approach achieves this connection by presenting real problems that require and exploit theory, physical reality and the skills needed to manipulate data.

This is <u>not</u> a strange idea. It was exactly this kind of linkage which led to the methods of inquiry now used by scientists and engineers (we call it the scientific method). Richard Feynman elegantly underscored the importance of this linkage when he virtually ended the arcane scientific debate about the cause of the Space Shuttle crash. He required neither tables of 9-digit data nor a multi-million dollar mainframe computer. He simply put a piece of O-ring material into a cup of ice water.

The reality-testing of theories is undoubtedly <u>the</u> central activity of real science. Problem-Solving Situations offer students solid experience in this activity. Scientific and mathematical concepts are, after all, only formalized interpretations of what goes on "out there." We can forge an understanding of this relationship by calling upon students to confront the kinds of problems and situations that demanded a deep predictive understanding of the natural world by scientists, engineers, and mathematicians.

Furthermore, Problem-Solving Situations give students opportunities to practice the skills they will need in the real world. One of many studies, for instance, recently summarized the mathematical expectations for new industrial employees in this way:[1]

- The ability to set up a problem with the appropriate operations, since most real problems are not well formulated.
- Knowledge of a variety of techniques to approach the problem.
- Understanding of its underlying mathematical features, and the ability to see—and believe in—the applicability of mathematics.
- The ability to work with others on such problems.

Problem-Solving Situations directly address all of these needs in a powerful and coherent way., Using this approach, students learn that:

- Problems usually need to be re-formulated before they can be solved.
- Multiple methods are not only inevitable, but encouraged. The problems naturally encourage students to bring previous experience to bear on each new situation. They must decide which experiences are relevant.
- The connection between mathematical techniques and scientific concepts and their utility in solving problems is direct and concrete, not at all abstract.
- Working in small groups is a powerful way to attack problems.

Of course, there are some interesting implications associated with a real problem-solving approach. This kind of learning must be structured so that success is defined by practical result rather than by a check against authority or answer key. After all, Euclid, Archimedes and Feynman did not "ask the teacher" if their answers were correct—they checked prediction against experience.

This kind of learning eliminates classroom teachers as taskmasters and ultimate authorities. In a world where physical reality is the ultimate decider, teachers are no longer the keepers of "the answer." They no longer decide when a problem is "done."

---

[1]Henry Pollak. Notes from a talk given at the Mathematical Sciences Education Board, Frameworks Conference, May 1987 *as cited in Curriculum and Evaluation Standards for School Mathematics,* National Council of Teachers of Mathematics, 1989, p.4.

Who Can Use This Book?

This book is a collection of 47 Problem-Solving Situations. As a teacher, you are the best judge of the suitability of a problem for your class, but I believe that teachers of grades 5-12 will find these most useful (the wide age variation here reflects both the flexibility of the problems and the huge spectrum of math and science skills that we encounter in the classroom).

These problems have been used successfully with children, adults, and adolescents of widely different levels of conceptual and methodological skills. But to be successful, each problem had to be modified to fit the dynamics of the groups asked to solve it. The problems in this book are not likely to be effective if used "as is"—like recipes in a cookbook. Cookbooks depend upon standardized ingredients and measurement standards. Students are considerably less regular than vegetables, eggs, and flour.

Your success in guiding your students through an inquiry-driven educational universe absolutely depends upon your locating the right level of paradox with which to force the students to link observation and explanation. This level is never the same from group to group, nor, for that matter, even from day to day.

This absolute need to interpret and tinker according to the diversity of the students may stop you right here, but it is the key to successful use of an inquiry-based approach.

Indeed, these problems are ideal for groups with a wide range of backgrounds. All of the problems were designed to be solved by groups. Further, they encourage real collaboration by demanding skills beyond any individual in the group. In my classroom, disparate skills and levels of understanding and experience absolutely required cooperative effort. Seen in this light, my students' differences, rather than becoming obstacles, served as tools that promoted elements of socialization as well as academic progress.

More importantly, however, these varying levels of skill and understanding reflect the world outside of the classroom—where real problems are solved by real people. Problem-solving outside of school is not conducted in groups where everyone commands the same skills and experiential base. It involves no rules except those imposed by contextual reality. Cheating as it is understood in schools (combining resources and knowledge) is an unreal and idiotic notion in the world outside of school. Out here, many paths are "allowed," and anyone can contribute to a useful solution. There is no premium paid for "extra" or solo work—within limits, we use whatever means are available to us when we are confronted with problems.

Virtually any kind of math or science class can benefit from Problem-Solving Situations. But you must understand that using such an approach will require many adjustments on your part. Expect a lot more noise, a lot more mess, and a lot less predictability than what you are probably accustomed to in your classroom. Also, expect some changes in the way that you and your students relate to each other. Your role, your authority, and your level of involvement in student work will all be affected.

If you're the kind of teacher who is ready for this kind of change, read on...

How to Use Problem-Solving Situations

Before beginning even the next paragraph, flip to the problems. They are the book. Skim though them in any order—be non-systematic. The clearest picture of the problem-solving approach is found in the problems and accompanying teacher notes. Questions concerning application, benefits, details, pedagogical issues, and difficulties of the method are all addressed there. If you're still interested in using these problems after a look, return to this page (hopefully with informed conviction and purpose) and continue....

You're back. The implementation of Problem-Solving Situations can be broken into five phases:

- Preparation and Planning
- Presentation to the Class
- Problem-Solving in Small Groups
- Evaluation as a Class
- The Next Step

And let's now look at the particular challenges presented by each phase....

I. Preparation and Planning

Choose a Problem. Don't worry about using problems out of order. In fact, the order presented here is simply an organizational convenience. Consider instead what each problem asks in light of where your students are.

Choose a problem that interests you and lends itself to something that your students are having difficulty with. While you don't want a problem that absolutely depends upon missing skills, you do not want to be timid in your choice either. Resist the temptation to select something too easy. Instead, choose a problem that will provide a challenge and involve some real discovery. Tossing your class an unrealistically easy problem may be a great way to attack social issues. But if this is your initial agenda, you may instead communicate that social interaction is the purpose of science class and thereby emasculate the activity of its integrity.

Good first choices involve simple equipment and logistics. Scissors, string and measurement of the classroom, for instance, are very less apt to fail than are operations involving multiple blindfolded groups linked by walkie-talkies over large distances. Consider, however, the level of sophistication and complexity necessary to grab your particular class. You must initially hook students into the process—and exotic and complicated problems do offer something for the extra work and risk that they require.

Some other general pointers:

Young groups often do well with problems that involve counting lots of little things. And water is unfailingly intriguing, though often messy.

When in doubt, the speed and distance problems are always good starters for anyone, including adults. They take science out of the classroom and immediately establish that this is real-world stuff.

Modify the Problem. In all likelihood, you'll need to alter just about every problem. Customize. Use wood instead of paper. Break one activity into two sessions. Ask students for written methodologies. Trade simple objects for complicated ones. Reverse the order or change the tone of presentation. Fit the problems to your situation and your students. You can't very well ask your students to work creatively and flexibly if you are rigidly bound by your own fears and needs for predictability.

As you modify the problem, ask the following questions:

- How should you use the groups? Should you have several groups working on all parts of the problem, or should you divide the tasks between groups? Which groups are likely to have trouble? What will this activity look like?

- What equipment do you need? Can you get enough pieces of key equipment that multiple groups can have access to it without bottlenecks? Are you depending upon someone else to provide a critical piece of equipment (or transportation) on a given day? You will learn the importance of this consideration the first time everyone is ready to go, after days of preparation and anticipation, and the stopwatch is left at home.

- How much time should you allot for each segment of the problem? Do you need to modify it so that it fits into your classroom and/or curricular schedule? Can you reasonably divide it into multiple days? Will you have time for an unscheduled follow-up problem if the need arises?

- Are there special things you can do with your class to add a special sense of excitement and/or motivation?

Gather the Equipment and Materials. There's a large materials list on Page 32 that covers all of the problems. But notice that it's divided into sections: *Essentials, Serious Needs,* and *Ridiculous Luxuries*. Also, realize that part of the impetus behind the development of these problems was my own profound shortage of science equipment—and I don't think my situation was unique. Even without a highly-developed scrounging capacity, you can acquire the entire *Essentials* list for $150 or less.

Remember, too, that you can start without any more than the materials you will need for a few initial problems—so there need be little or no expense at the beginning.

When you know you'll be doing a lot more of this sort of thing, bite the bullet and get yourself a **triple-beam balance**. It's used in more than half of the problems. You may be happy borrowing one as needed for a while, but unless you can keep it in your classroom for an extended period of time, you'll lose some hard-to-recreate teaching opportunities. In my classroom, some of the best learning to come out of this approach occurred on the "wrong day"—the day after problem-solving. "Hey, this is sort of like what happened when we were working on that problem yesterday" is tough to pick up on if you can't pounce when the thought is alive. It's a lot to give up for want of a $70 piece of equipment.

Also, stress to your class that even what may look like a collection of junk is valuable to you *and to them*, not only for its utility in the classroom, but for the expenditure of time and effort that has gone into its collection. Whenever possible, you can obviate this explanation by enlisting students in equipment acquisition. But don't count on everything arriving on the day of destiny. Make sure you build in some lead time to account for poor memory, missed rides, or equipment that arrives in less-than-advertised condition ("It worked OK at my uncle's last Christmas").

Try the Problem Yourself. If possible (it's not), try every problem before offering it. Even the simplest presents unforeseen obstacles. Think about how many kids will be doing what, and when and where they'll be doing it. Consider all of the intangibles that you know better than anyone else. You know who will need coaxing, who will be a leader, and who will begin heading for the nurse's office with a stomach ache 5 minutes before science period. Play out how your students will react to being asked for one answer or two. Plan for the kid who is never chosen to be in a group. Think about the one who cannot use fractions.

Of course, I was never totally ready, and you won't be either, but you can work to be alert and flexible as events unfold.

II. PRESENTATION TO THE CLASS

It's usually a good idea to convene the class as a group before breaking into small groups. There are (at least) three things that you need to do here:

Present the Problem. Present the problem or challenge orally, using a small demonstration if necessary. Choose your words carefully: you don't want to bias the choice of methodology that will be used.

Before handing every student a written copy of the problem under attack, consider this: In my experience, it was rarely a good idea to hand out more than 1 copy per 5 kids. Limiting the number of "official documents" always promotes communication and interdependence in a group. Even the lonest loner wants to know what's happening.

This is when you build your final agenda into the structure of the activity. Assigning two groups the separate parts of a larger problem will produce one kind of result; something else will happen if you assign the same two groups separate responsibilities to solve the same problem. This is when you commit to one scenario or the other—and it's when you find out what you forgot to consider ("What are we supposed to do if *they* hog the pipette all the time?").

Explain the Ground Rules. Clearly spell out the limits of what behavior you'll tolerate and establish a consensus about this. Clearly describe your role in the process: What kinds of questions will you answer—and what will you be doing while the groups are working? The class must know how it will be evaluated (see *Evaluation as a Class*, page 28)—and that you won't say "right" or "wrong."

Explain any special rules governing the problem, and make sure that all equipment is available and that any guidelines for its use are clearly understood. What you say here is carved in granite. When kids reach points of frustration (i.e. key moments of learning), they will remember every syllable that escaped your mouth: "You said no rulers; you didn't say anything about yardsticks."

Establish the Margin of Error. Most of the problems include a blank *Margin of Error* heading. The Margin of Error is a key criterion for the "correctness" of a solution—that is, how close to the actual tested value does a prediction have to be in order to be "correct"?

Once again, the definition of success or failure here lies outside of the teacher. While it is true that, as a teacher, I had enormous power to set such limits (whether I wanted it or not), it was essential to involve students in the process. In most cases, the margin of error was negotiated right here—after the problem was presented. My experience has been that students are no more likely to seek ridiculously liberal performance standards than are their parents and teachers. Teachers do not look for jobs that pay for unproductive busywork. We value ourselves partially as a function of what we do and how well we do it. We owe our students the same opportunity to choose high standards of performance—and the risk of failure that comes with the package.

III. PROBLEM-SOLVING IN SMALL GROUPS

Nitty-gritty. For the most part, your active role is over, but your behavior as a teacher is critical. You need good mental preparation and a clear idea of your mission. Otherwise, the number and variety of demands that unfold can overwhelm you in what can seem to be—or truly become—chaos. It is essential that you build a framework of expectation that will allow you to tell the difference between productive exchange and bedlam.

Your New Role. Depending upon your agenda(s), group, and the problem, your proper role in this process can vary tremendously. In general, however, it should be significantly less prominent than the role to which you are accustomed. If you want to help, consider doing so as an "outside expert" who can be used only if properly and clearly directed by student "clients." Remember that by the 4th grade, most students are generally quite expert at assuming dependent, passive roles in school. When I allowed such passivity, it was only a short time before I found myself once again in my traditional role of "he who holds the bag." I got "the answer" while they waited for 3 o'clock to roll around. Rhetoric alone does not redistribute responsibility. If you can do so with genuine interest—rather than as someone making sure that everyone is working and progressing—wander around and find out what different groups are doing. Ask them if they've seen what's going on across the table (usually they haven't, especially if they're really involved in what they're doing.)

Groups. Groups don't necessarily mean chaos and bedlam, but they do mean talking, movement, unpredictable events, and mess. This approach to math and science is based on kids learning to regulate their own learning and discovery—and it doesn't usually happen overnight. When I first tried these problems, I had to make a serious emotional commitment to the idea—even if only for a few hours a week—to obtain more than a headache for my efforts. This was more difficult than it sounds. It meant surrendering my power in the classroom—power I had spent years developing.

Collective group efforts offered something to me that was enormously valuable, but they presented significant dangers as well. The group is an ideal format to work out many academic and social issues, but it's a risky proposition for the insecure student. A positive group can turn into a predatory animal or a negative exercise in frustration with little visible warning. There is a narrow muddy path between freedom and anarchy, between creative space and the license to injure others. I learned (painfully) to become invisible and unfelt. At the same time, I had to cultivate the ability to remain in absolute touch with what went on from a distance. It was difficult yet crucial for me to remember that my students were uniquely exposed and vulnerable as they went about their work in new terrain. I needed to be careful not to make them dependent upon my praise lest its absence be taken, unintentionally, as criticism. I had to learn to encourage instead of praise.

Despite the significant risks involved, this approach to learning was probably the best vehicle I ever developed for integrating "difficult kids" into my own classroom. A model of learning that valued individual contributions without depending upon them in a frightening manner was often just the ticket for kids who were otherwise unable to "find the way in."

Temptations to Avoid:

- *Do not give hints to weaker students.* Hints imply that you know the answer and that your student can't find it without you. Not only is this usually wrong, it builds student dependence. Encourage *all* students to pursue their ideas until they can decide if those ideas are sound or not. When students are completely and disastrously befuddled, redirect their confusion and need for help to other students.

- *Avoid fostering rumors—through some mysterious process—that you favor one group's approach over another's.* You must preserve your role as Keeper of the Ground Rules and shed that of Keeper of the Knowledge. This takes conscious effort on your part; kids will not make this separation naturally or without practice.

- *Do not pretend to know more than you do.* You do not have to play games and pretend to know (or not know) things. It's still all right to decide if and when to release information, but your students should come to appreciate that you are going through your own learning process and that you, too, will make mistakes. And there is absolutely nothing like the look of a kid who realizes that his or her approach was not only not wrong, but superior to yours. If you use these problems honestly and with commitment, this will happen. All of my students have solved problems that, at one time or another, adult groups were unable to conquer. (Did you know, that the perimeter of a circle will not define an equivalent area if reformed into a square? I didn't, but a 14 year-old who doesn't know multiplication facts proved it to me.)

- *Avoid giving up on the problem when some unforeseen error occurs (often your responsibility).* Acting as a role model—showing how to cope with unforeseen obstacles—is one of your most important roles in this entire learning process. Go ahead and change the rules or parameters of a problem if you run into an unforeseen glitch (the stove isn't working; the little tray leaks, etc.) but *do not bolt* any and every time things do not proceed exactly as expected. You must tolerate some frustration (yours and your students') and assess its depth and implications before you decide that it's unproductive, negative, or needful of your action.

- *Do not ignore your own ground rules to be kind.* Consequences promised beforehand must follow consistently and without animosity. Presumably, your students will have agreed during the presentation that they're responsible for obeying the ground rules, that the consequences that result from a transgression are their fault and not yours. In formulating the rules, be careful that you have only as many as you truly need—and that you can enforce them.

- *Do not expect perfect behavior to follow directly from good motivation.* Generally speaking, motivation to solve these problems will be fairly high. But don't expect to see one of those progressive education scenes rapturously described by pedagogical experts who have never been in a classroom. It is rare that everyone within a small group of self-directed learners becomes deeply involved in absorbing discovery for three hours. This will happen, but it's like seeing a shooting star. Savor its beauty and try to be in the right place to see more. Don't give up at the first attempted eraser hockey game or discussion of last night's TV show. Think how an office of generally productive adults looks, take a breath, and count to ten.

  Remember: while you should not and cannot suspend your responsibility to maintain a safe and productive classroom, you are shifting some of the burden to your students. If you panic and end the project at the first sign of trouble or difficulty, you tell your students that this is not science, but an odd game that you'll try if they're good (and end if they're not).

What If They Can't? A tricky but common situation is the small group with a great idea or strategy, but no ability to pursue it because of poor math or other problems. Develop whole-number approximation strategies with them ("What's the highest it could be? The lowest? What's in between? Which is it closer to?"). Work on the skill with them, not the larger problem. That's theirs to chew on.

Another reasonable thing to do is simply suspend operations on the problem with one or two students who are marooned by whatever skill deficit it is that has sunk their strategy. Work with them on the fractions, percents, or whatever it is that has halted progress. After all, this is an ideal opportunity—they have seen their own need to learn how to use the same fractions that may have represented purposeless torture the day before (this will also give you a way to be a productive citizen and stay out of everyone else's hair).

IV. EVALUATION AS A CLASS

This is payoff time for the students and for the learning process. At a minimum, the class should collect their predictions and then determine the "answer" by brute measurement. Ideally, however, there are some other things that might happen after the predictions are made, but before they are tested:

Present the Problem-Solving Strategies. Each group should be given the responsibility to present its prediction(s) and to describe orally to the rest of the class the procedures and strategies employed in determining it. Each group should be expected to make a persuasive case for why its methods will yield a good prediction. Depending upon your agenda, it may also be appropriate to charge each group with the responsibility of demonstrating that its method is better than another. Questions should be encouraged from fellow students. You, the teacher, should remain non-committal here, although you might ask the students to consider whether their answers are identical, highly different, or largely similar. Engage a discussion about whether differences stem from procedural or conceptual issues.

Evaluate the Strategies. Once all presentations and discussions above have been completed, you might wish to do a formal evaluation of the problem-solving strategies. Not all classes will benefit from this. Some may be creatively inhibited by being "evaluated." Others will be more motivated and will benefit from giving and getting formal feedback. One good way to do a formal evaluation is to have *other* students (those not in the group being evaluated) publicly rate the effectiveness of the strategy on a scale from 0 to 5. Remember, they are rating the strategies before anybody knows for sure how good the predictions really are. (This is also an opportunity to introduce some statistical concepts: What is the fairest overall rating to give a strategy—the mode, median, or mean of the individual ratings?)

Develop a New, Coordinated Class-Wide Prediction. It is often a good idea to have the class arrive at a new, consensus prediction based on the predictions of the individual groups and all of the discussion about methodology. They might use a weighted average (with the subjective ratings of methodology acting as the weights), or graphical interpolation, or other some other method of their own devising.

Test the Prediction. This is the moment of truth. All of the calculating, hypothesizing, and posturing gets exposed to the harsh light of reality. *Weigh* the thing (or count it, measure it, etc.)—perform the test. Be sure to involve the students in this process as well; generally there will be no shortage of volunteers. Now comes the opportunity to discuss the value of repeated trials and of the inevitable uncertainty of measurements. It will be obvious that actual, physical *data* is different from abstract, idealized numbers.

V. AFTER TESTING THE PREDICTION: THE NEXT STEP

Okay, it's weighed (or counted, or measured). Success or failure at the assigned task has been determined. You know how close each prediction came to the actual value and whether it was "close enough." This is the time to bring up your observations about group process, good and bad things you have seen, evaluations of effort etc.

Failure. The solutions for all of the problems in the book are reality tests. In general, with a little bit of defining structure, students are left free to solve a testable problem. In this approach, <u>you must allow failure</u>. While repeated and undifferentiated failure is always tough, kids can handle quite a bit more than we give them credit for *if* they are given some control of the process and goals toward which they struggle. It's time to repeat an oft-mouthed cliché about "learning from failure," but in a new spirit: Failure is an absolutely essential component of all real science. For that matter, it's an element of all real learning. If you take failure out of the process, you are not doing science. Worse, you are eliminating learning.

If your students have failed to solve the problem within the agreed upon limits of accuracy, explore the failure with them. Give them a stake in deciding what went wrong and how (and if) to re-approach the meat of the problem at a later date. Do *not* accept, "yeah, we get it—when's lunch?" This is initially very hard ground and requires a persistent commitment to the process on your part. When a group fails, it is important not to gibber on about their "good try," but to enlist their effort in the location of the error. In most instances of this sort, it is productive to ask the students how to retest their understanding of whatever it was that beat them. This is *real* science: technique, procedure, and hypothesis must be revaluated before picking up again. If you persist in reinforcing this approach and attitude, you should find your students assuming responsibility for their own work by Spring vacation.

A related point is your own failure. Trust me—regardless of your intention and preparation, things will go wrong. Equipment will fail; a key student won't come to school on the critical day; you'll fail to understand the phenomenon being investigated.

Do not hide your own failures from your students. This is an important reality to model: If you can't fail publicly, how can your students do so? After an initial panic and anger that "the teacher don't even know," most students come to see such difficulties differently. They realize that they are doing significant work, work capable of engaging and frustrating an adult. This—more than any other factor—instills an invaluable flavor of cooperative effort into the approach.

Success. If your students are succeeding with the problems more frequently than about 70% of the time, you may be making things too easy. Tighten the margin of error—or throw in a whammy. Select more difficult problems or concentrate on known conceptual, procedural, or skill weaknesses. If you cannot reasonably make the problems more challenging without simply playing tricks, explain the situation to your students and ask their help in creating new problems either for themselves and/or you. Bring in an outside dungeonmaster—a "guest puzzler."

Clean-up. Don't forget to allow time to clean-up, disassemble, restore, and—in some cases—return to the classroom.

Getting Your ... Stuff Together

Essentials:

- A motley collection of bolts, nuts, screws, paper clips, ball bearings, BB's, pennies, nails, washers, etc. (i.e. the back shelf in your garage)
- Alcohol
- Bicycle wheel
- Bottles, cans, jars, buckets—anything that holds liquid—preferably of simple shape.
- Boxes of plastic, wood, or metal
- Calculators
- Canning wax
- Cardboard, posterbaord, heavy sandpaper
- Chalk
- Compass (drafting) (2)
- Drafter's triangle
- Electric drill
- Elmer's glue
- Exacto or single-edged razor blades
- Eye dropper
- Graduated cylinder (100 ml)
- Graph paper (1 cm. units and smaller)
- Hand tools
- Hanging lab thermometer (with both °C and °F)

- Heat source
- Masking tape, glue
- Motor oil
- Opaque bottles with screw-on lids (3)
- Paper towels
- Pipe cleaners
- Pipettes (1 and 5 ml)
- Plastic hose
- Rods: wooden, plastic, metal
- Rubber bands, string, and wires
- Rulers, metric/Eng. (4)
- Salad oil
- Saucepan
- Scissors
- Scrap wood
- Tacks
- Tape measure (25')
- Toilet paper
- Triple-beam balance
- Volumetric flasks (2) 100 ml
- Watch
- Wax or clay
- Wire cutter

Serious Needs:

- Aerial photo of your town
- C-clamps
- Coins (50-1,000)
- Compass (field)
- Computer with word-processing software
- Deines (or similar) math blocks, sizes from 1 to 1,000 cc's
- Digital watch
- Electric motor
- Extension ladder (30')
- Graduated cylinders (50 and 150 ml)
- Inner tube
- Level
- Plastic containers (rectangular, conical, cylindrical) to hold water
- Playschool balance
- Protractor
- Rope
- Rubber balls
- Slinky
- Snow rake handle or other extendable pole (20' or more);
- Springs
- Strainer
- Tape measure (50')
- Tape recorder
- Topographic maps
- Toy phonograph
- Tracing paper
- Turkey baster
- Wax

Ridiculous Luxuries:

- Binoculars
- Digital stopwatch
- Laser range finder
- Microscope
- Polaroid camera
- Sugar Pops
- Videocamera and VCR
- Walkie talkies
- Wheeled distance measurement tool

Getting Your ... Stuff Together

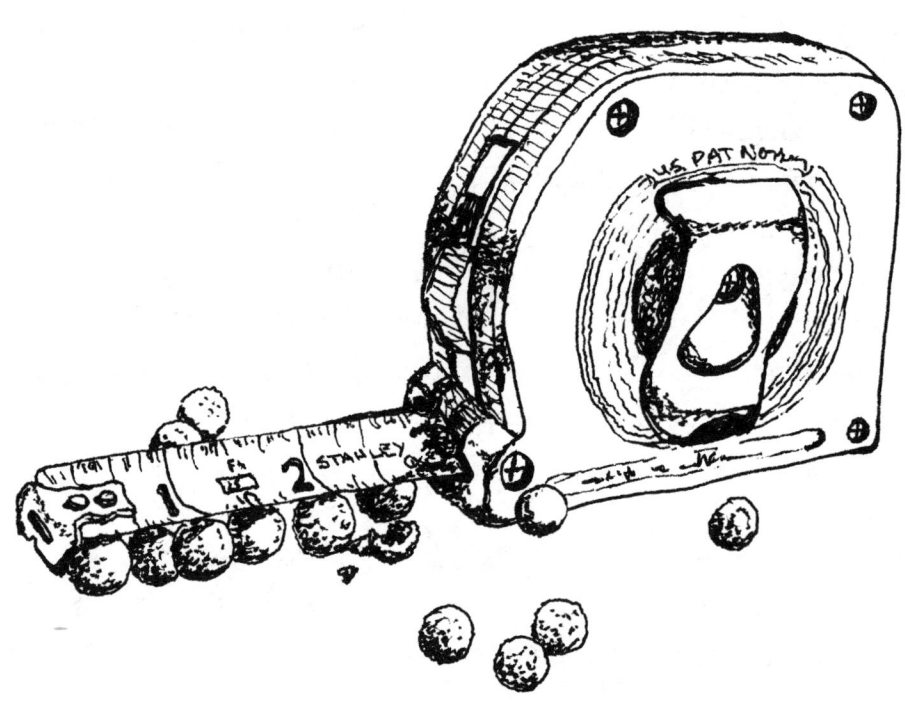

I. Length, Number and Weight

Section Notes

The problems in this section generally introduce students to issues of measurement and technique without requiring sophisticated interplay between concepts. Students will encounter the notion of determining the size of unknown constituent parts by examining their relationships to composite quantities. Also, they will begin to think about essential and extraneous information, accuracy, and useful units of measurement. There are a number of good starters here, particularly for students with low math concepts and confidence levels.

Problems 1, 3, and 6 are proven "ice breakers"—generally solvable even by beginning groups with little experience working together. Problem 6 also raises some crucial issues of methodology and of working as a group in an almost totally non-threatening way (so it's actually swell for stiff adults at workshops, too).

Problem 2 generates thought about estimation (although it can be presented with a small enough degree of error to promote other skills at a later stage of work.) Unlike other problems in the book, your students may have encountered other versions of it in other places. This shouldn't in and of itself "ruin" the problem, but be prepared for, "I did that in Mrs. Smith's room last year." Also, some groups can march through this one pretty quickly; plan accordingly with a backup activity.

Whether through doing problem 4 or by some other means, it is advisable to thoroughly ground students with the idea that 1 cc. of water weighs about 1 gram before working on other problems involving liquid, volume, and density. Problem 4 is also good for introducing thought about errors of technique, relative degrees and limits of accuracy, and the value of predictable methods and equipment.

Problem 5 is difficult for groups with no understanding of cubic centimeters and milliliters. This problem can be easily directed toward estimation skills if time limits are imposed and the degree of accuracy is chosen to promote a more approximate process of determination.

Problem 7 was included as a glorified word problem—for reasons explained in the teacher notes. You can use it to gently expose students to another kind of problem solving, or to reground students who might have been moved too quickly toward an unfamiliar approach.

1: The Doodah

Problem: In front of you is a doodah made of 3 pennies, a piece of wood and a washer, tied together with a piece of string. You also have another penny, a second washer, and another piece of string. How long is the piece of string holding the doodah together?

Details: In order to determine your answer, a person from your team may weigh the doodah *once*. Other than this, you cannot touch it. You are free to do whatever you wish with the loose doodah components.

Margin of Error:

Teacher Notes:

This is a fairly straightforward problem—an easy one to use as an introduction to the inquiry approach. It hinges on 2 ideas:

1. The weights of the individual pieces of a collection of items add up to its total weight. While this is perhaps obvious, its utility is not always recognized by students. This kind of problem moves kids to think about what they know and what they don't know, and how both of these pieces of information can be useful to them.

2. A uniformly constituted object's weight will vary directly with its length (actually its volume, but since the cross-section of any length of string is essentially identical, it can be thought of as a line segment.)

A reasonable margin of error for a beginning group is ±3 cm.

Special Materials:

- The doodah: "Doodah" is neither a misprint nor what Camptown Ladies sing all the livelong day. Doodah is a term generated by students which gradually came to describe any object created specifically to torture them during science activities. The first doodah was created with washers, coins, and string. Subsequent doodahs relied heavily on scrap wood and Elmer's Glue. Yours can be made of whatever is practical and appropriate to the task. Write me in care of the publisher if you develop the Molybdenum/Titanium Doodah of the 21st Century.

- Other than extra component materials, students will probably need little beyond basic classroom supplies and a triple-beam balance to attack this problem. It is *always* good to have graph paper and math blocks around.

Spinoffs:

- At a later time, this problem—like most—can be easily deepened by cranking up the accuracy expectation. This will inevitably lead to exploration of differences between seemingly identical objects and ways to deal with those differences (what if you weighed 2 pennies and used their average weight? What if you used 10?). These are not questions, however, that *you* want to ask. Instead, simply make the problem require a more complex methodology by demanding more accuracy. You can also ask if there is a limit to the level of accuracy attainable with whatever method has been developed by the group.

- The general question of margin of error, of course, can also lead to the idea of limitations presented by equipment and materials. A commonly available triple-beam balance, for instance, is not generally capable of anything beyond .1 gram accuracy (.01g for the fancier ones). String is not only irregular in its construction, but in its stretchability. How do you know that your length measurements are really accurate?

2: Paper Stack

Problem: Without unfastening the tape or undoing the bundle of paper in any way, figure out how many pieces of paper are in the stack.

Details: You may not "fiddle" with the stack in any way. You may measure it, weigh it, etc., but you may not count the sheets. You may use anything (or anyone) which might be helpful, but not more than 3 other sheets of paper. When the groups have agreed upon one answer—and everyone in either group can explain how that answer was determined, we'll break the tape and count the sheets.

Margin of Error:

Teacher Notes:

This is a fairly easy problem to solve, with many variations appearing in teacher magazines and activity workbooks. This version is designed to promote cooperation and communication between kids. The format is usable for any problem, but it can backfire where really threatened kids refuse to participate or can't grasp the explanation or thought processes of their classmates. In such cases, instead of promoting group identity, you can wind up with an angry group and an alienated scapegoat despite the best intentions of everyone involved.

A reasonable margin of error is 3 sheets of paper. Even better is 3 sheets *per 100*, which will move your class toward a more useful percentage-based concept of accuracy.

Special Materials:

- A large stack of paper; masking tape

- For students: Nothing Unusual. Although the three lists in the Materials Section of the book are an indication of what my classes used to solve these problems, "Nothing Unusual" will come to mean some specific—and probably different—combination and/or uses of the "usual stuff." It is convenient to store the "usual stuff" in one place, on a shelf or in a box(es), for instance. In this way, kids help define what "usual" science materials are—and learn to think of things like graph paper, rulers, and scissors in a new light.

Spinoffs:

1. Limit groups to the use of *part of one sheet* of extra paper (this pushes the group to consider area/weight rather than number/weight relationship).

2. Have one group decide how to attack the problem and make them responsible for explaining their method—in writing—to another group which is responsible for collecting the data and doing the calculations.

3. Tape 1 of 3 coins (penny, quarter, half-dollar) inside the stack and ask group to determine which coin is hidden inside. Note the amount of tape you use.

4. Tape 2 coins (out of the same 3 possibilities) in the stack and require group to determine which are there. Again, give them the tape length.

5. Wrap a 100-sheet paper stack so that the paper can't be seen and allow groups to use only 5 sheets each of 3 different kinds of paper to determine which kind of paper is in the stack.

6. Wrap a stack of an unspecified number of sheets and follow procedure for spinoff #5.

3: Toilet Paper

Problem: Determine the length of the toilet paper on the partially used roll—*without removing or unwinding any of the paper from the roll*. You may not remove the rubber band that wraps it, either.

Details: You will also be given a full roll of toilet paper containing 200 sheets (according to a label, which you don't get), also wrapped with a rubber band. The full roll may not be unwound, either. Finally, you get a rubber band like the one which wraps the two rolls and an empty cardboard tube like those inside of both toilet paper rolls.

You may also use any tool that might help (if available), but you may not leave the room nor use any other toilet paper, labels, rubber bands, or toilet paper tubes.

After you have determined the length of the roll, we will unwind the mystery roll and measure its length together—but not until everyone in your group can explain the reasoning behind your estimate. Part of your task will be to decide how close you think you should be able to get to the actual length.

Margin of Error:

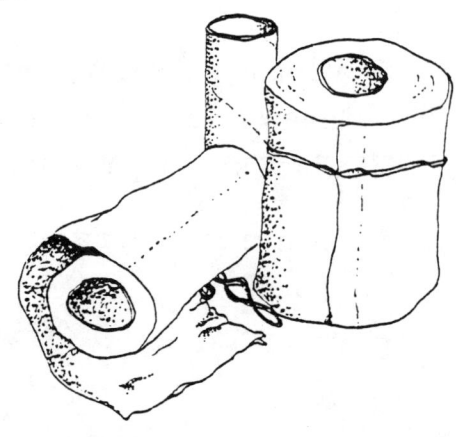

Teacher Notes:

This is a good starter problem because of its simplicity, and the fun and richness of measuring the length of the paper when it is finally unrolled to determine the "answer." Simple but important concepts about recording data consistently come up as the hundred odd sheets of paper have to be unrolled and kept track of.

It's probably not necessary to overdo matters with charts, but it can be quite interesting to have 2 kids or groups count and measure. Some multiply one length by the number of sections, others use a tape and add measurements. Either activity can reveal problems which can be pointed out by using the other method for comparison. The multiplication method is quick, but a small error multiplied many times because of one poorly read measurement or oddly sized piece will be magnified. Adding many measurements increases the likelihood of calculation errors and forces conversions and regroupings of units—and it takes longer and is harder if the fractions aren't convenient. All of this can lead to discussion of ways to combine strengths of different methods (e.g. measure a few sections and multiply an average length by the number of sections.)

The most compelling convincer of authenticity is a 50' tape measure used in a space large enough to allow the whole roll to be unwound and laid out flat. This is also probably the most reliable method of measurement because of fewer variables—one reading only, no calculations. There are still questions of where the exact end of the tape is etc., but these are generally irrelevant unless the margin of error is very tightly limited.

Similar to Doodah #1, this nevertheless looks different because of the obvious, visible area of a section of toilet paper—it's not like string; it's "fat." Some groups spin their wheels because of this and do a lot of unnecessary (though not irrelevant) work calculating the area of one section and relating *area* rather than length to weight. This is unnecessary only because the thickness and dimensions of each piece of paper are relatively uniform. The problem can obviously be attacked with the same concepts needed for #1.

If, however, you are lucky enough to have 2 groups that solve the problem, one using area calculation and one using only length, you are well positioned to develop a discussion or activity around what makes data useful or not for a given task. In one such instance that I treasure, one group which took twice as long as another (the second group didn't bother with the area calculation) was absolutely stunned that the answers of the two groups were essentially the same. Even more interesting was the fast group's belief that their result wasn't as good because they hadn't done as much work. This is rich stuff for discussion and other activities.

A reasonable margin of error for a beginning group is about 2 feet.

Special Materials:

- Two identical brand rolls of toilet paper, one whole and one partially used; identical rubber bands; triple-beam balance.

- Students will require Nothing Unusual, although a 50-foot tape measure makes the final determination a little more direct and dramatic. This is particularly advisable if you're dealing with kids who think that you're the sort of teacher who would purposely "overmilk" an activity rather than let justifiably impatient students see how they did.

Spinoffs:

1. Use 2 rubber bands on either roll with same objective.
2. Allow no direct measurement of paper with tools made for measurement purpose.
3. Instead of asking how long the roll is, ask where it will end if laid back and forth across the room or a table.
4. Combine spinoffs #2 and #3.

4: The Weight of Water

Problem: You have two tasks: First, find out the exact weight of 100 ml. of water at room temperature. Secondly, determine the weight of 1 ml. of water at room temperature.

Details: The flasks you will be given are called volumetric flasks. They are made to accurately measure 100 milliliters of liquid. This amount of water at room temperature takes up 100 cubic centimeters of space (think of 100 of the small blocks: each one is a cubic centimeter because it is 1 centimeter in each direction.)

When one of these flasks is filled with water so that the bottom of the dip in the water line just touches the top of the painted line on the neck of the flask, that's very close to exactly 100 ml. of water in the flask.

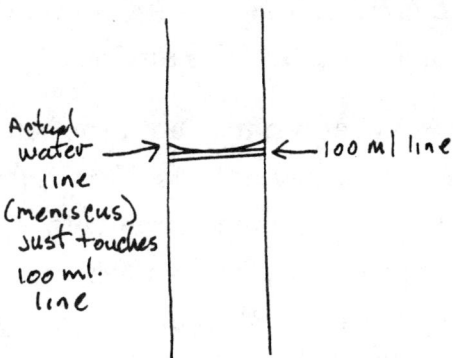

This problem is not difficult, but you need to be very careful to get accurate results. Since you're interested in a very small weight, think about things that might throw off your measurements. *The flasks and pipettes are also expensive, so be careful with them.*

Margin of Error:

Teacher's Notes:

This problem is closer to a traditional lab than most, because the specific fact that 1 ml. of water weighs approximately 1 gram is very useful. A key fact, it can be profitably repeated 2- or 3-thousand times a day until it is second nature for every student in your class to think about it at the mere mention of water. Water is a terrifically regular, volume-filling, and available material with a known weight that's easy to remember (the numbers are easy because metric weight is based, after all, on the weight of water). It's easy to understand volume with the idea of "how much water it would take to fill this space?" If this relationship and visualization are firmly grasped, they can be used in countless ways.

The problem departs from the format of the rest of the book in that its explanation and the problem itself require some special equipment. There are ways to explain or demonstrate what a cubic centimeter is without math blocks (you can even make them if you're a masochist), but the blocks are an invaluable tool in many of these problems and a great concrete referent in general—get them if you can. Volumetric flasks and pipettes are also very handy for many purposes. 2 flasks and 4 pipettes (1 ml and 10 ml) can be purchased through supply houses for under $20 if there aren't any rolling around in your building. Get the lowest quality (but glass, not plastic). It's unlikely you'll need anything more accurate.

This problem is probably important to do before others involving water. In any case, early in the game, you need to encourage kids to think about procedural things that could make their measurements of liquid inaccurate. Talk (or elicit talk) about drops on the side of containers, the balance pans, etc. Involve them in thinking about how to weigh only that which they intend to weigh ("Do you dry this or not?" "When?" "Why?") Any of these questions can lead to side-experiments or problems to determine the relative importance of a procedure in a given situation.

The non-explanation of room temperature is a purposeful shortcoming (the relationship of temperature to liquid volume is the subject of later problems). On the few occasions when I've been asked about it at this stage, I've played over-obviously dumb ("Gee...I'm not sure I remember—maybe you can find out about it"), which has stimulated not only dismissive laughter but some interest ("Hey you guys, that must be important or he wouldn't act so weird about it").

Special Materials:

- 100-ml volumetric flasks
- 1-ml and 5-ml pipettes
- Math blocks
- Tissues and paper towels (or Q-tips) for swabbing droplets off of the flask necks
- Lab thermometer (just in case)

Spinoffs:

1. Compare weights of different liquids.
2. Ask groups to identify different clear liquids by comparing the weights of equal volumes of each liquid.
3. Ask groups to identify different clear liquids by comparing the weights of *un*equal volumes of each liquid.
4. Speculate about whether such determinations are equally difficult with large and small volumes of liquids.

5. Pennies in a Bottle

Problem #1: Determine how many pennies are in the bottle. You may not open, turn upside down, or shake the bottle. The only other money that you can use are the ten pennies and the dollar bill on the table. There are exactly (within .1 g) 100 grams of water in the bottle. The bottle itself weighs _____ grams when empty.

Problem #2: How many milliliters of water must you add to the bottle to make the whole thing weigh 500 grams?

Margins of Error: Problem #1: 1 penny
Problem #2: 10 ml. of water

Teacher Notes:

Again, the problem requires the use of the relationship between what's known and what isn't. In math, you'd say, "If $a+b=c$, then $c-a=b$ and $c-b=a$." This idea is needed to find the total weight of the pennies (and the additional water needed.)

The number of pennies is best determined by dividing their total weight by the average weight of one penny. Although they get 10 pennies to encourage the use of an average, some groups will use the weight of a single penny. Unfortunately, this sometimes works just fine, but over several problems where they use one item rather than an average, they'll have trouble. It's a good thing to learn through failure or through different results by different groups—and over the long haul, the methodology of using averages will emerge more strongly if you let it come out on its own; the simple presence of 10 pennies may light a few bulbs. Also, you may or may not want to hammer at the idea of a *mathematical* average. Kids can come up with a reasonably good average of 10 weights by looking at them in a list.

The dollar bill is thrown in as a not-very-subtle hint that not every piece of information in a situation is relevant. Few kids will be fooled by it, but that's not the point; it's there to make them think about the issue. And an even nastier related idea suggested by the bill is that some situations may not contain *enough* information to be "solved" or understood within constraints presented.

I usually present this problem in an *opaque bottle* with a screw-on lid, but on occasion, it's been useful to present it in a transparent bottle, to encourage straight guessing, volume estimation, thought about packing behavior, and other interesting issues. Things go best then if different groups attack the problem differently, allowing comparison of the advantages and disadvantages of each (depending upon the accuracy needed, the visual method can be better if speed is essential.)

When you fill in the weight of the bottle used, round to the nearest .1 g and be sure to include the weight of the cap.

Special Materials:

- Identical capped bottles
- Lots of pennies
- One dollar bill
- Triple-beam balance

Spinoffs:

1. Include three dollar bills in the bottle.
2. Use a different-looking liquid with a very different density (cooking oil is nice for a good mess.)
3. Use a seemingly different liquid with virtually the same density as water (e.g. dyed water.).

6. Kix Are For Kids

Problem: How many Kix are in the unopened box? To solve the problem, you may use an empty Kix box and a small pile of Kix. You may *not* open the unopened box, nor use cereal other than what you're given. You may use anything else that you think will be useful in this vitally important quest for truth.

Margin of Error: ±8% of the actual number of Kix counted when the box is opened.

Teacher Notes:

This is a good starter problem for groups not fully formed because of the fun of the counting process at the end. As you'll discover, it's not easy to count a lot of little pieces of cereal with a group of kids. Piles tend to get missed, messed, or counted twice. Record-keeping systems come about out of necessity, rather than by direction. A lot of issues about behavior in groups emerge as well ("Well, *why* didn't anybody hear you when you said how many were in your pile?").

Problems of what to do about crumbs and partial pieces and issues of consistent observation methodology become crucial here. This makes the problem fertile ground for thinking about not only average items, but how problems are defined and framed (e.g. what exactly *is* 1 Kix?).

The 8% margin of error is liberal enough to allow reasonable chance of success and yet introduces another way of thinking about the entire accuracy concept ("Is this *way* off or not?" "Compared to what?"). It's also a good way to introduce the percentage concept ("no more than 8 off for every 100 Kix that are in the box"). Obviously, this could be introduced into any problem—or left out of this one.

Special Materials:

- Two boxes of Kix, one full and unopened, one empty
- A handful of loose Kix
- Some smaller boxes or rectangular containers

Spinoffs:

1. Use Sugar Pops.
2. Count out 300 intact Kix and predict how much of a graduated cylinder they'd fill if crushed (or soaked).
3. Retype the instructions with spelling, punctuation, and usage errors, and stipulate that a successful solution includes the correction of the directions. This wrinkle is especially good for involving confirmed 'non-science' types, but be careful to make sure they're not allowed to overspecialize their way out of the rest of the problem.

7: Wood

Problem: You have one piece of wood. Can you answer the following questions about it without cutting or damaging it—and without using any other wood? Any other methods are fair (but you have to pay for any long-distance phone calls). Round off your predictions to whole numbers.

1. How much will a 1-foot-long piece of this wood weigh?

2. How much will a one-inch-long piece weigh?

3. How much will 4 feet of it weigh?

4. Draw lines on the wood for where to cut pieces that will weigh:

    a. 88g
    b. 44g
    c. 20g
    d. 10g

    After you've drawn the lines, we'll saw the pieces and weigh them. You've done a good job if you can get within ___ grams of the actual weight of each piece.

5. The price of the wood is ___ cents per foot. What did the whole piece of wood cost? You should be able to get within 3 cents of the price, which is on the actual sticker in my pocket.

Teacher Notes:

Obviously, this is a much more structured and traditionally formatted exercise than most of those in the book. While it still leaves some elements of attack strategy up to the students, it guides them in a pretty heavy-handed way along a certain path.

This problem is included for a few reasons. First, it acknowledges that there are different levels of readiness for dealing with open-ended problems. This problem was developed for a group of kids who had consistently been frustrated by a combination of poor math skills and lack of confidence in dealing with problems whose answers weren't known by the teacher or listed in a book.

Secondly, it's a good example of how the kinds of things taught in the other exercises can be taught in other ways. The inquiry method, if insisted upon as **The Way** to teach every thing to every student can be just as tyrannical as any other unthinkingly applied methodology. Kids need to deal with open-ended inquiry based exploration, but not all the time and not always in the same way. Some need the security (occasionally or frequently) of more familiar-looking work.

The problem itself is straightforward enough to require little explanation. It's a good foot-wetter and consolidator. If you live in a state with a sales tax, you'll have to modify the whole thing. Watch out for boards of inconsistent density. These would include composites or boards with knots. And finally, during the check process, when you're sawing, you can save yourself a lot of grief and embarrassment if you (or the students) think very carefully about which cuts to make first.

Special Materials:

- About ten feet of wood (boards or stripping) *that is uniform* (a lot of seemingly identical boards are made from different density wood—*check*)
- Saw
- T-square, framing square, or other tool to lay out 90 degree cuts

Spinoffs:

1. Repeat the exercise with a double-width (or double-thickness) board and impose a time limit on the predictions.

2. Put some of the cut-up pieces in a sealed container of known weight and ask how long a board the hidden pieces will add up to when laid end to end.

3. Repeat spinoff #2 with an egg added into the container.

4. Repeat spinoff #3 with a broken egg added into the container.

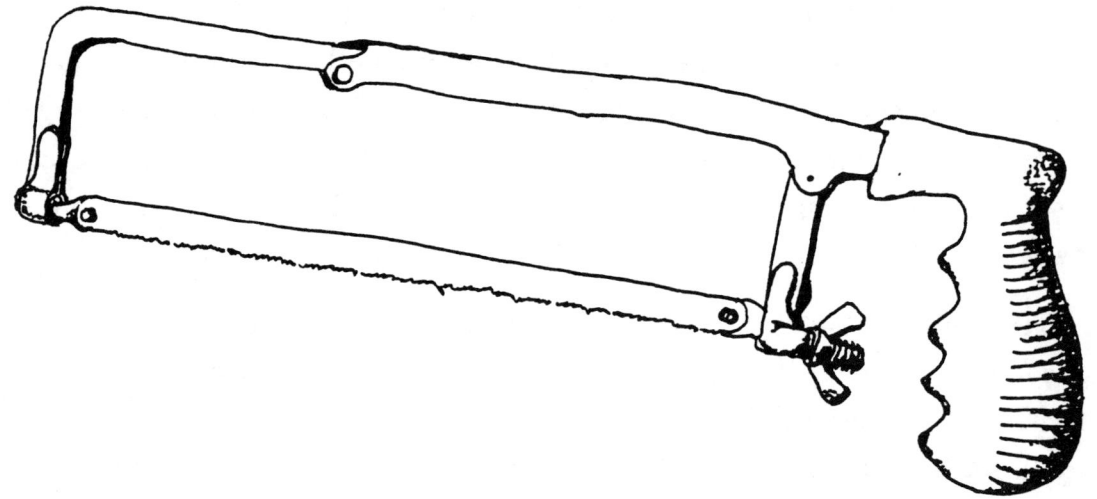

Notes (Yours)

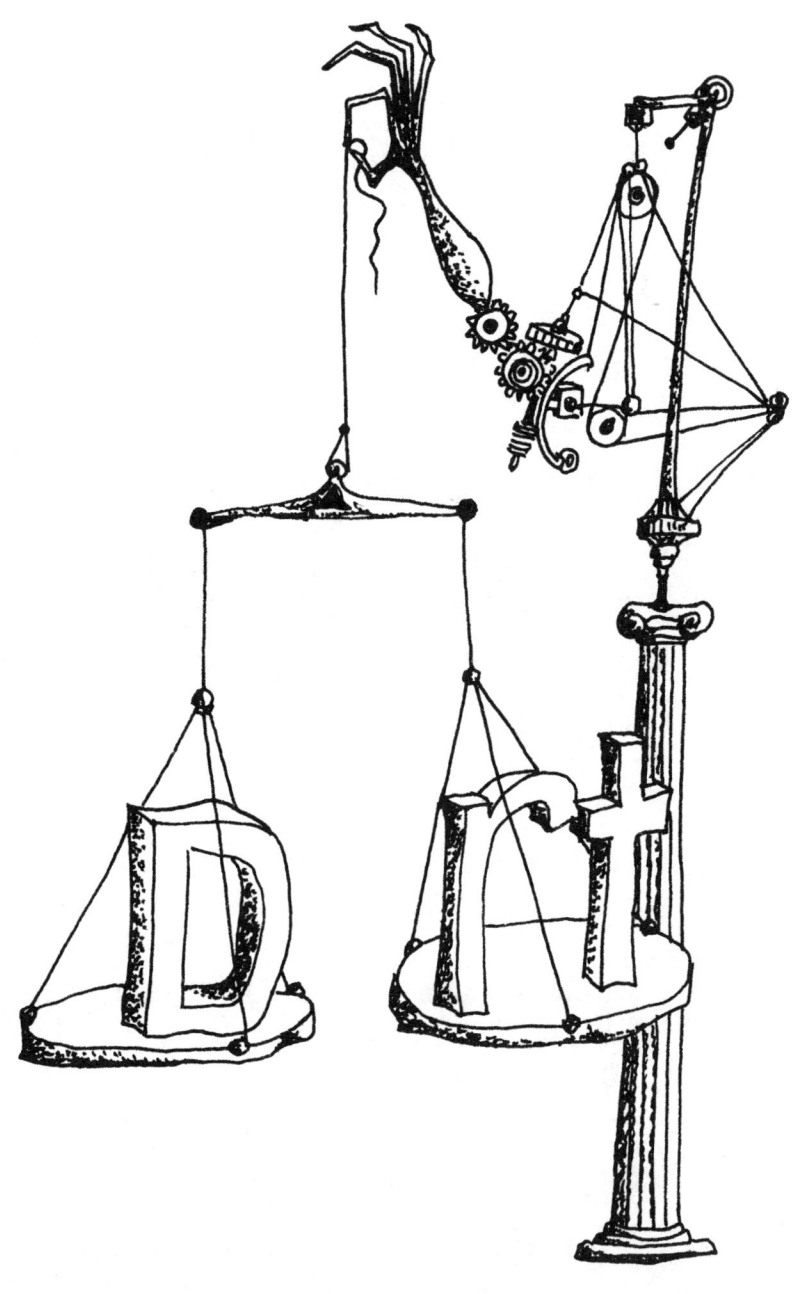

II. Speed and Distance

Section Notes

The problems in this section involve the interplay between Distance (D), Speed (R for rate), and Time (T). Most of these are little different than what is found in the average bad math book—except they call for real measurement rather than simple paper calculations. That's not a trivial difference. It forces students to think about what is reasonable in the world that they live in—rather than the abstracted world found on a piece of paper.

Perhaps the most valuable aspect of these problems is their almost total reliance on accurate, planned observation techniques. The inclusion of such a dynamic variable forces students to deal with the kinds of observational limits and logistical hassles that scientists deal with routinely (the comet passes by *once every 70 years* and it doesn't stop). So it's best to think about what to measure before it arrives and it's best to assign tasks in a way that the right things will be observed and recorded when the opportunity occurs. This means planning, teamwork, theory—and interpretation of often imperfect data.

Most of these problems require travel outside of the classroom and a 1- to 2-hour block of time. This presents obvious logistical problems, so you'll probably need to modify some situations. Since these problems rely on the real world, however, they can't be generically fitted to all situations, anyway. For example, those written here are site-specific problems developed for Concord, New Hampshire. You'll need to change them to fit your geography, time structure, and institutional constraints.

When you make your modifications, remember that, on the whole, *big* distances (beyond a 1-time tape measure value) add a new and valuable dimension to the problems. A large distance forces a real-world flavor and brings up considerations of measurement techniques. A 16-foot tape measure or a yardstick, for instance, is just not an easy way to measure 3.8 kilometers. And cars *do* have to stop for traffic lights, and people *do* trip over curbs sometimes. It rains. And curbs, bumps, and trees *do* get in the way and change measurement readings.

These factors are not obstacles, however, but opportunities. They are the real-world events and conditions which characterize the richness of real science. Use them, and enjoy them.

8: Unicycle Walk

Problem: Predict the distance that Joanne will cover when walking at a steady speed for 25 minutes. You may use any measuring device in the classroom, but you cannot use <u>anything</u> other than the unicycle to measure between the 2 chalk lines on the sidewalk in front of the building.

Details: I'll time Joanne with a stopwatch to see how long she takes to walk the distance between them (after she has reached a steady walking speed). But she won't stop then; she'll continue from the moment she crosses the first chalk line until her watch indicates that she's walked 25 minutes. At that point—wherever she is—she'll stop, mark her position with a piece of chalk, and wait to be picked up. One recorder from each group will be in the car to verify the odometer reading.

Margin of Error: 0.05 miles of the actual distance, as measured by the odometer on the car which picks her up.

Teacher Notes:

Okay, so maybe a unicycle isn't that easy to come by—a bicycle wheel will work equally well. The problem is a fairly simple determination of speed which is then used to extrapolate distance travelled in 25 minutes. The main difficulties are with unit conversions and the requirement to use big ugly numbers that don't work out nicely, thus making it easy to lose sight of where one is in the calculation process.

If you have broken your skull trying to get your students to label their results, a problem like this can provide an exquisite lesson. When 8 kids each spend 40 minutes producing 2 pages of numbers and then don't know where or why their answers differ, someone usually becomes exasperated enough to look for a method that will allow cross-checking. If not, you can massage the situation by requiring agreement among answers and explanations of how they were arrived at. This can be a brutal introduction to the idea of consistent units (the odometer measures miles; the ruler, centimeters) and a lesson in which units are easier to use when.

Special Materials:

- Unicycle or bicycle wheel
- 2 Stopwatches—one for walker, one for you (a cheap digital watch with a timer feature is OK for the walker)
- A one- or two-mile route that will allow a steady walking speed
- Vehicle with odometer
- A spare adult (or pre-planted vehicle) to pick up the walker

Spinoffs:

1. Joanne will stop walking for 2 minutes and 14 seconds at whatever point she has reached after 9 minutes and 13 seconds of walking.
2. How many telephone poles will she pass?

9: Driveby

Problem: You'll have one opportunity to watch Joanne drive by an observation point (OP) overlooking the interstate. Bring along whatever you will need to accurately predict how long it will take her to reach the Manchester city line.

Details: The city line is 18.2 miles away from the caution sign at the OP, as measured by the odometer on Joanne's car. She will pass the OP at approximately 10 a.m., driving at a steady speed. You have one hour and 15 minutes to decide what you'll need and how to use it before you get on the van to go to the OP. You will then have approximately 5 minutes at the OP before the Joannemobile drives by. The actual time taken for the trip will be determined by a student timer using a digital watch and riding in the car with Joanne.

Margin of Error:

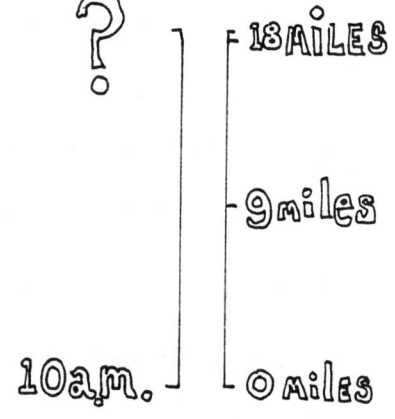

Teacher Notes:

This problem, more than anything else, is a group communication exercise. It requires that students agree on an effective observation procedure within a limited amount of time. The once-only nature of the driveby forces forethought and visualization of the calculations to be done after the car disappears from sight. Knowledge about what the freeway roadside is like (mile markers, fence posts) can make unlikely contributors to group strategy. It is amazing how rarely anyone attempting this one thinks to bring along two easily visible objects to mark off an interval along the roadway. There are huge numbers and lots of conversions. This is very rich ground for delegation of responsibility and coordination of results.

As such, the problem contains a distinct danger of deteriorating into chaos, conflict, or underinvolvement by many who goof off while a few masterminds do the work. Of course, this problem can occur with almost any of these situations, but this is a good point to think about it if you haven't already done so. Various strategies can be employed to head such difficulties off at the pass. A drastic but effective one is to require separate answers after explaining that you will allow and encourage discussion before the driveby, but eliminate it afterward. This Draconian approach encourages sharing of ideas because everyone needs to know what's going on before the observation in order to get his or her own answer at the end.

Special Materials:

- 2 Stopwatches—one for the student timer, one for the class (a cheap digital watch with a timer feature is OK for the student timer).

- A safe viewing spot from which to watch a car drive by on a fairly long (10-30 mile drive.

- A route with easily determined end points of verifiable measurement (mile posts, town lines, etc.).

- Bus or van

Spinoffs:

1. Predict time of their return as well (not as easy as it seems).

2. Allow no watches or official timing instruments at OP.

3. Allow no official measuring devices at OP.

10: Twenty-Minute Walk

Problem: Predict how far Joanne will walk in 20 minutes. On your representative's signal, she will start from the white chalk line and walk at a steady pace toward town on State St. She will not stop or start over once she has been signalled to start. You will be able to observe her from anywhere in the parking lot.

Details: You may use objects for measuring. You may not use any "official" distance-measuring devices, such as rulers, tape measures, yard-sticks, etc.

Once you have decided how far Joanne will get in the 20 minutes, you must somehow determine *where that spot is* and mark it with a piece of chalk. But before you do so, your group must decide how close your prediction should be in order to be considered successful.

Margin of Error:

Teacher Notes:

This is a great one for a nice spring day. The sight of 15 or 20 kids laying down lengths of string or lying down end-to-end like a leap-frogging machine—for a mile or so—quickens a perverse heart. And though I've never seen a group that didn't complain about the childish stupidity of this problem, I've never seen one that didn't enjoy it and learn something, too.

Of course, this is another exploration of the utility of manipulations possible with distance, time, and rate variables. But it offers a lot more: It really teaches the value of thinking about scale before determining what measuring device to use for a task. It also provokes thought about what a measuring device is in the first place. And it really pushes group cooperation and consistency in procedure.

Since it's generally a good experience, encourage a lenient margin of error (25-50 yards). Make sure that your walker can exactly locate his/her stopping point in a way unnoticeable to the approaching string-layers or leap-froggers. Usually, if the walker carries a tape measure, paper, and pencil; the distance can easily be noted as a distance from some landmark. Discuss this with the walker ahead of time—being unable to find the stopping point does not go over well with the troops.

Special Materials:

- 2 Stopwatches—one for the walker (a cheap digital watch is OK)
- Unicycle or bicycle wheel
- A nice day and a lot of time
- String, rope, boards—anything "unofficial" to measure distance

Spinoffs:

1. Specify a really "convenient" measuring device—like a 6-inch ruler (don't try this unless you have a solid relationship with your class).
2. Eliminate the use of watches or clocks for everyone except the walker.

10: Twenty-Minute Walk

11: Untimed Walk

Problem: Predict how long it will take Susan to walk to the store. On a signal from your group's chosen Master Of The First Step, she will start walking at a steady pace until she arrives at the newspaper machine (closest end) in front of the store. She will click on a stopwatch when she passes the start line in front of the school and click it off when she passes the newspaper machine. How fast she walks is up to her, but she is paid by the hour.

Details: Once she has begun walking, you won't be allowed to leave the parking lot of the school. You may use whatever or whoever might help you in your task, but you may not use any device made by others for the purpose of measuring distance (rulers etc.). Before we accept your group's estimate, every member of your group must be able to explain how you arrived at it.

Margin of Error: 30 seconds

Teacher Notes:

This is a straightforward solving of the D = RT equation for T, once the group realizes that they must establish D and R through observation and measurement. Of course, it's made a bit tougher by the stipulation barring measurement devices.

The mention of "whatever or whoever might help" is included in a lot of these problems. Some teachers have suggested that students might use this loophole to cheat by asking another adult for help or—in this problem—enlisting the aid of an outside student to record the time of the walk.

Fine. Although kids mention such possibilities with great glee, only one group in 2 years ever tried such a thing with me—and in both cases, the experience was invaluable: They had to figure out who to call and explain their purpose and needs over the phone. They had to synchronize watches and describe how to measure some ridiculous distance with which I had been torturing them. Not only is this more legitimate science (use what is available), it forces an identification and classification of information that is an important objective of virtually every science problem. One of the 2 instances involved a long string of phone calls to city offices and bureaucrats; the other involved a parent in our science activity. Neither of these outcomes was in any way a problem from where I sat.

Special Materials:

- 2 Stopwatches (a cheap digital watch with a stopwatch button is OK for the walker).
- A nice day and a lot of time
- String, rope, boards—something to measure distance

Spinoffs:

1. To one group, hand out copies of the problem as written, and ask them to rewrite it for another so that it makes sense, including the names and places. Put the first group in charge of all your normal duties, including the check for total participation by the second group, who solves the problem.

2. Ask Susan to walk in a bizarre fashion—but still at a steady pace.

3. Ask Susan to walk in a bizarre fashion and *un*steady pace (and consider altering the margin of error if she's really creative and uninhibited.)

4. Make an audio tape which lasts 15 seconds exactly (not easy to do) and stipulate that this is the only timing device allowable in this problem.

12: Head On

Problem: Bill and Jenn will each carry a Walkman tuned to 89 FM. At the first mention of time after 9:50 a.m. on the station, they will begin traveling. Bill will ride his bike, as steadily as possible, toward town on North State St., starting from the chalk line in front of the school. Jenn will walk toward the school from the Gulf Station in town. Both will try to maintain a steady speed.

Your mission: Predict when and where they will meet.

Details: Jenn will record the time and location of the meeting, using her watch, a tape measure, a piece of chalk, and whatever landmark she can find to indicate where the meeting occurs.

Members of the group may be at school, at the Gulf, or in the bus—but nowhere else, until Jenn and Bill return to school. You need to identify who will be doing what and have the Gulf group ready to go by 9:30.

Margin of Error:

Teacher Notes:

This is an admittedly ambitious problem that I haven't yet presented to a group. I've even thought of including a group from another school as an observer corps (1 of the 2). While it suggests those "a-train-leaves-from-Chicago" problems that are the lowpoint of Algebra for most people, there are visual methods of scale comparison (from which the algebraic process was derived) that will allow its solution by a tenacious bunch of kids with a lot of drive. An aerial photo or very good city map might be nice to have around the room (without explanation). Also, in your initial presentation, make it clear that nobody travels on a public street with headphones on.

The problem is obviously quite difficult but might make a terrific final ordeal. Try it—and send your complaints/observations to the publisher.

Special Materials:

- Stopwatches
- Odometer
- Tape measure and chalk for one of the walkers
- Unicycle or bicycle wheel
- Two Walkman-style radios
- A nice day and a lot of time
- String, rope, boards—something to measure distance
- Bus or van

Spinoffs:

Since this is an as-yet unspun spinoff itself, it might be best to see how the problem works before jazzing it up with complications.

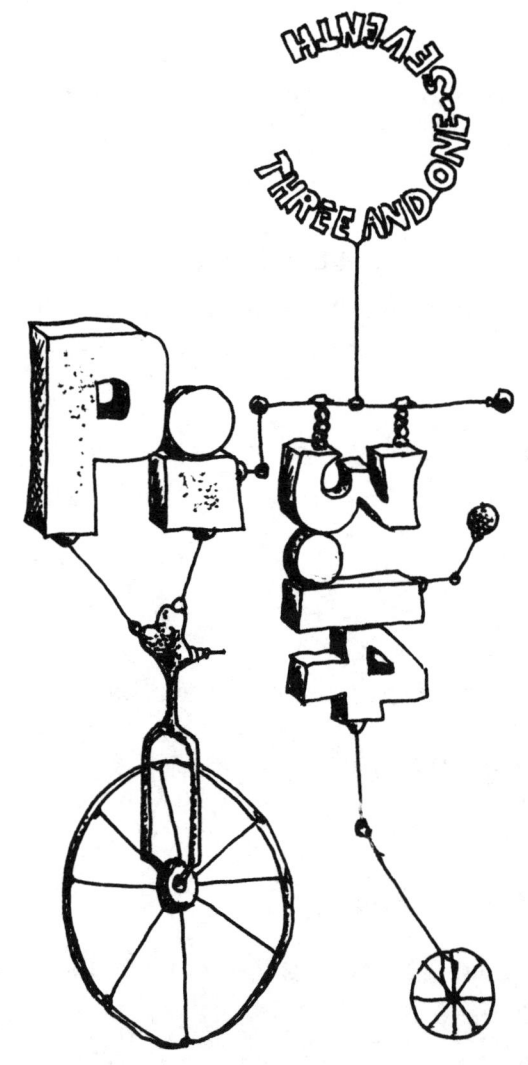

III. Circumference and Area

Section Notes

Most problems in this section explore the nature of *pi* (π), the number that describes how various components of the circle relate to one another. All of the problems can be solved without it, but as a group, they were designed to push students toward the idea that there must be easier ways of doing things than winding string around circles and gridding out circles with tiny boxes.

Some students who don't yet understand these relationships may have already learned the equations which describe them. Usually they're somewhat stymied by the need to inject nasty real-world measurements into the formulae, but they can be exploited as alternate-method checkers. Often, even though others in the group expect that the formula jockeys know what they are doing, final results of formula cranking are less than perfect (it's amazing how often kids will just multiply π by r^2 if they see a circle—regardless of the problem posed). Of course, if you have a group that truly understands the circle's relationships and formulae, just congratulate yourself on your own excellent teaching and skip this section altogether.

I wrote these problems without using the language of circles—to discourage reliance on formulae—but it's a good idea to introduce the terms when appropriate. Problem 13 is an easy starting exploration of the relationship of diameter to circumference. Many teachers use an inked-can or rolling-pin variant of this as a demonstration of π. In keeping with the spirit of this book, my version has a smaller-than-usual teacher role. Another version employs two teams, to stress multiple findings and progress toward a more formalized kind of knowledge.

Problem 14 emphasizes the role of modeling and its usefulness in different ways. Not only can simple models explain complicated problems, but sometimes we can use formalized knowledge and complex information to penetrate simple-seeming phenomena in front of our eyes. Students need to *feel* that (relevant) information can always be used to penetrate what's not understood in a situation.

Problem 15 is the heart of the section for me. I am amazed at the power of this kind of drawing when it is fully explored. This image gave me my first real grasp of the relationship at hand here. Spend some time with these drawings.

Don't decide five minutes before class to try problem 16.

13: Garbage

Problems:

Team A: How far across is a circle that will roll exactly 10 times from one side of the room to the other?

Margin of Error: 2 centimeters

Team B: How wide is the room if this garbage can lid will roll exactly ___ times around from one side to the other? Unfortunately, you may not lift the lid from the desk, nor measure the room, nor ask team A.

Margin of Error: 4% of the room's width

Teacher Notes:

Although most problems in this book lend themselves to separate teams, this version has two teams built into it: Essentially, Teams A and B do spinoffs of the other's circumference problem, because groups, always interested in what the other guys are doing, often cross-pollinate problem-solving strategies ("Hey look—they're measuring across the lid."). But this doesn't always work. Sometimes one group simply imitates the other with no consideration of appropriateness etc.

Most groups solve this kind of problem through **modeling**. They typically need string, graph paper, cans, bottles, ink, paint, scissors, and blocks—but be prepared for anything. This problem has elicited some truly innovative solutions!

Special Materials:

- Paper, cardboard, graph paper
- Compass
- Scissors
- String, tacks, chalk
- Rulers, tape measures
- Blocks
- Flat, round objects
- Garbage can lid

Spinoffs:

1. Without touching the garbage can lid or rolling any another object of the same size across the floor, predict how many times the lid—of known diameter—will go around when rolled, wall-to-wall, across the floor (1/4 turn is a good Margin of Error). No identically-sized objects allowed.

14: Around and Through

Problem: A 650-mph plane can circle the globe in 40 hours. The same plane could fly from one side of the planet to the other, through the Earth's center, in 12.7388 hours, if only there were a hole. How many times longer does it take to fly around the Earth than through it?

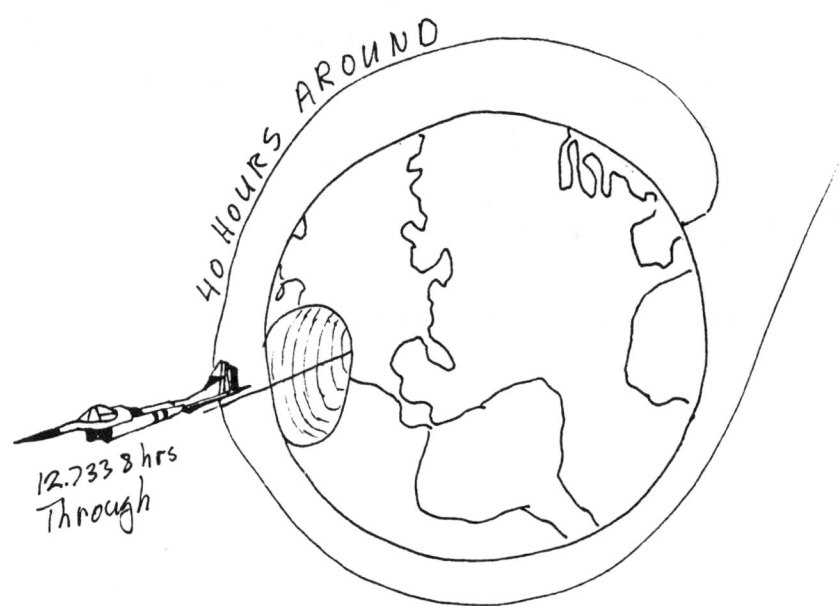

Use whatever you can find in this information to decide how many complete revolutions a bike wheel will take to cover exactly one mile. When you've got an estimate that you can trust and explain, figure out a way to record revolutions of the wheel accurately and roll it the number of times estimated along the street toward town. Mark your start and stop points. We'll use a car odometer to measure your estimated mile.

Margin of Error:

Teacher Notes:

This problem was born of too much success (or—looking at things another way—failure): My students had become so adept at *getting around* the actual formulae that they refused to use, discover, or acknowledge them. That is, they enjoyed—and didn't stray from—the effective but time-consuming strategies they had developed to work out circumferences and areas. They actually understood how circles worked better than many adults, but they never made the mental leap toward consolidation and shortcut that I had simply assumed would happen. My tightening the time constraints had simply caused frustration rather than suggesting a need for streamlining or for using π. Many groups have landed in this situation to some extent, and it's a common problem associated with an inquiry-based method. But in order to be practically effective, the kids' specific discoveries must somehow eventually lead them to a formalization of process.

Special Materials:

- Vehicle with odometer
- Bicycle wheel

Spinoffs:

1. Students, using a bike with an RPM clicker, predict how many rotations to a distant (about 1 mile) point, as indicated on a good map or aerial photo. (Will shifting gears make a difference? Why?)

2. Create 3 variants of the first part of the problem, present to 3 different groups, and ask everyone to be jointly responsible for finding any common feature of the 3 calculations.

3. After spinoff #2, groups create a definition of 3.14 that an outside (but sympathetic) engineer or mathematician will accept.

15: Boxed Wheels

Problem #1: The 3 drawings you have been given each contain a circle inside of a square that has been divided into 4 quarters. Divide into 3 teams, one for each drawing.

    a. What's the area of (how many little 1-centimeter squares are in) the large square in your drawing?

    b. What's the area of each of the quarters?

    c. What's the area of the circle? Estimate by adding the parts of centimeter units along the circle's edge.

Compare your results with other teams. Is there a pattern that might help you with the next problem?

Problem #2: On a piece of graph paper, use a compass to draw a circle at least 3 inches across but of a different size than any of those in the handed-out drawings. Divide the circle into quarters and draw one square using 2 of the lines which mark off one quarter of your circle. Your drawing should look like an unfinished version of the handed-out drawings, showing one square with 2 of its sides inside of the circle. Use the area of this quarter box to predict the area of the whole circle.

Problem #3: Estimate the *weight* of the circle that is drawn on the back of the cardboard square. You may not cut the square or use any other cardboard. When the entire group agrees upon an estimate of the circle's weight, we will cut it out and weigh it. If you can get within 5% of the actual weight, you know what you're doing.

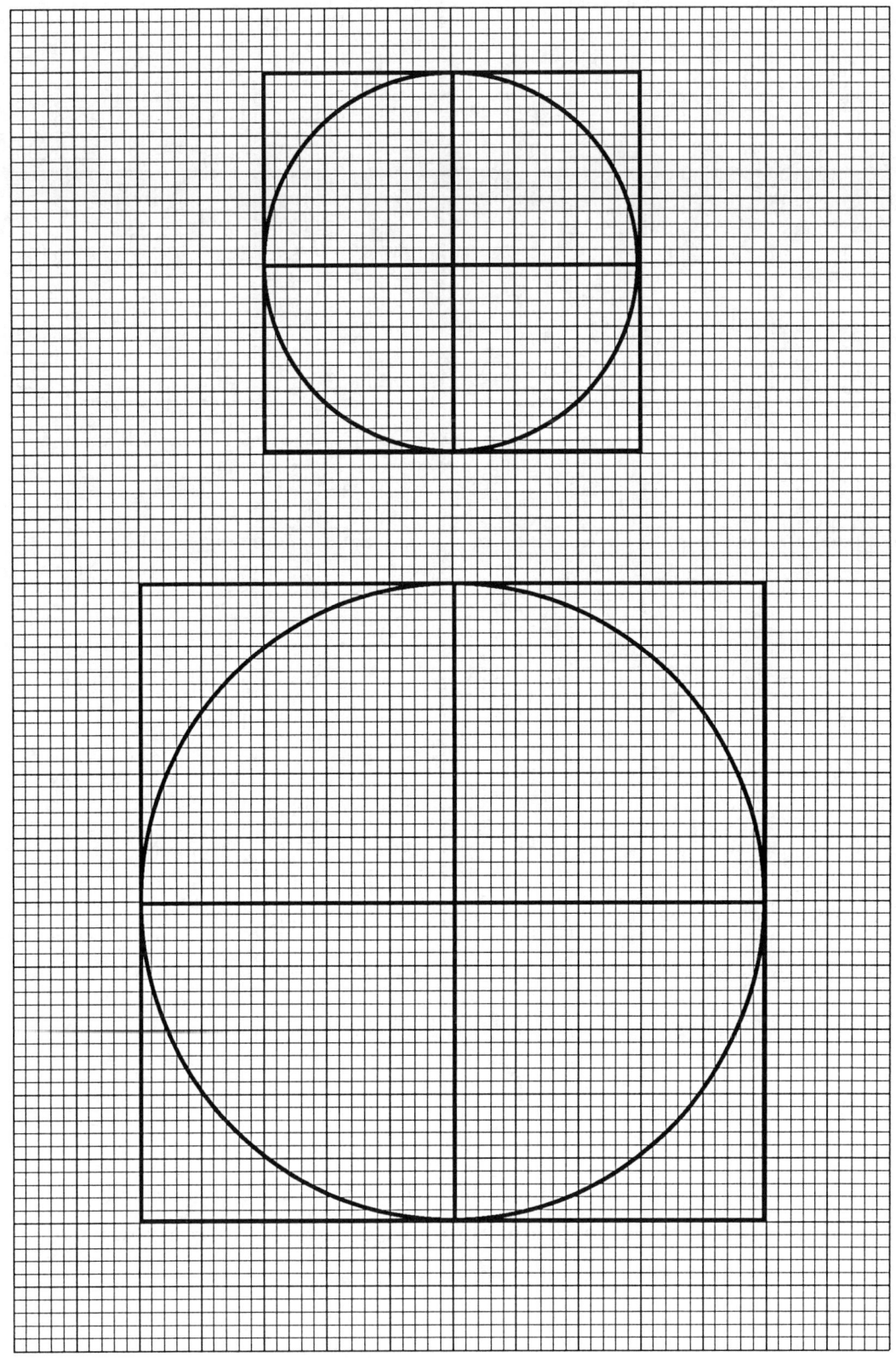

15: Boxed Wheels

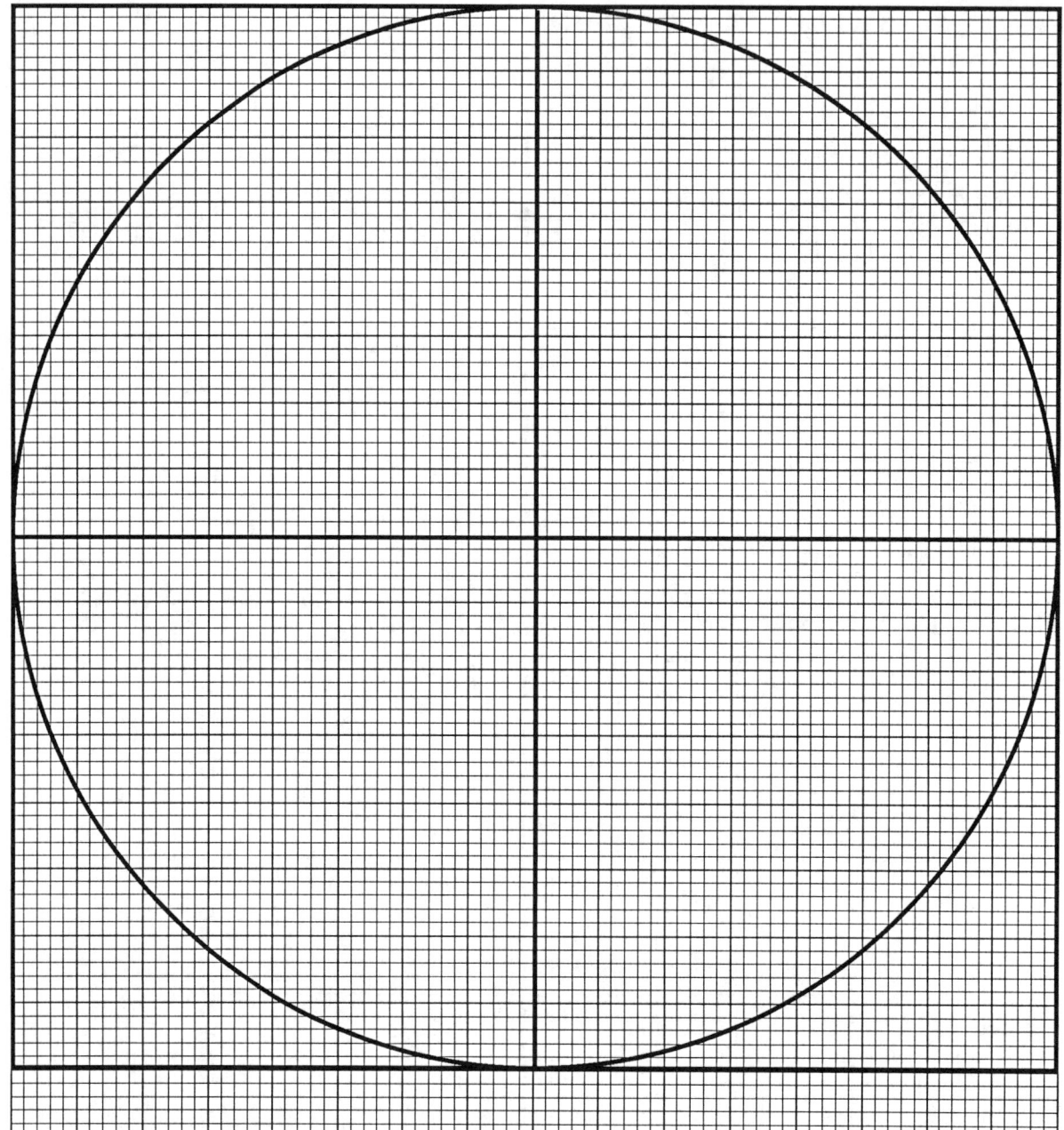

Teacher's Notes:

A nifty problem, this allows a lot of participation and contribution by kids of widely different skills. Some groups that go through this exercise discover that a circle is a fixed percentage of its surrounding square. Others find that the r^2 quarter, if multiplied by 3 and a seventh, always equals the area of the circle that is surrounded by 4 of the r^2 boxes. Some decide that 21.4% of the large square is not in the circle that it surrounds. And some groups see only that the circle is a little more than 3 times the area of the r^2 box. But all groups, in my experience, made it to the point of being able to reasonably estimate the area of a circle.

A key to maximizing the value of this problem is some way of sharing methods. Though I haven't been universally successful in bringing students to the realization that these methods are all expressions of the same truth (a constant ratio of circumference and area to radius or diameter), it's always valuable to try.

Special Materials:

- Clean copies of the drawings (make extras)
- *Lots* of graph paper and math blocks (almost essential here)
- Triple-beam balance(s)
- Cardboard
- X-acto knife or single-edge razor blade
- Lots of squares cut from various materials that can be drawn upon (consider who gets the ones with nice even-numbered measurements and who gets the ones that are 8.37 cm per side).
- Lots of compasses and pairs of scissors

Spinoffs:

1. Ask students to figure out a way to chalk-line a perfect circle that touches each wall of a *square room*. Then, after circle is drawn, ask them to calculate its area by counting floor tiles. Then use the circular area information to determine the length of each wall.

2. Students are asked to predict the weight of an unavailable (to them) square piece of cardboard based on the weight of a round piece which would be surrounded by it and touch each side. The round piece is the only cardboard available to the students.

16: In and Out

Problem: Each of you will be given a square piece of paper, sandpaper, posterboard, or cardboard—each of a different size. First, find the weight and area of your square. Next, carefully draw a circle that just touches the outer edge of each side of it. Then draw lines dividing the square into 4 equal parts. Finally, cut the circle out.

Does the circle weigh more or less than the square? Compare the weight of the two shapes as a percentage. What percent of the square is the circle?

Reassemble the pieces on the table so that you have the large square formed again. Cut out one of four small squares and weigh it (it will be in two pieces because of your circle-cut, but that's OK). How many of the smaller squares would equal the weight of the whole circle?

At this point, you should have:

1. The weight of the big square
2. The area of the big square
3. The weight of the circle
4. The percent of the square's weight found in the circle
5. The area of a quarter of the big square.
6. Your estimate of how many of the little squares it would take to equal the weight of the whole circle.

Use whatever you need of all this to find the area of the circle. Try to prove that your result makes sense.

Teacher Notes :

This particular version of a basic exercise requires a lot of work on your part, since you have to prepare a different square for each student. Ideally, these squares should be large enough and of heavy enough materials that the relative weight differences between pieces will be well within the scale's range of accuracy. In some instances, I also went to the effort of ruling in 1-centimeter grids on at least part of some squares before handing them out (though for other groups, it was enough to have a pad of graph paper conveniently and prominently hanging around the classroom).

The aim of this exercise is twofold: First, we want kids to apply a wide variety of methods to the idea of circular area. Secondly, we want to collect a lot of information about how circular area relates to area of the particular squares generated by circles.

A way to further gel all of this is to collect all of the class's numerical results (numbers 1 through 6) on the board in some kind of grid. Then work the students for what they notice: Are there any numbers that seem to show up frequently? Does this mean anything useful? Can they come up with a theory about comparing squares to the circles that fit inside of their edges? Were they able to determine the areas of their circles? How did circular areas compare to the areas of the big squares? How did they compare to the areas of the little squares? Hammer away on common results. You may have to work on some students to see that some data, while not precisely identical, may be in good agreement (e.g. 3.12, 3.14 and "about 3 times").

On the basis of this discussion, ask your class to devise a theory about the relationship of every circle to the square that surrounds it that everyone can accept and understand. Or, ask them to come up with a theory about the relationship between the areas of circles and the *small* squares that everyone in the class can accept and understand.

Offer some kind of prize or reward for anyone who can disprove either theory over the course of the year. Leave them up in a corner of your blackboard or on a wall until and if they can be successfully challenged.

Special Materials:

- Squares of different sizes and materials that can be drawn upon and easily cut with scissors, one per student.
- Graph paper and math blocks
- Compasses (as many as you can get)
- Triple-beam balance(s)
- X-acto knives or single-edge razor blades
- Lots of pairs of scissors

Spinoffs:

1. Hand out slips with the weights of yet unmade circles (one per pair of students) written on them. Then hand out pieces of various material (cardboard, tagboard, manila paper) to each pair and ask them to cut out a circle that will wiegh the specified amount.

2. Same as #1, but specify that the material may be cut only once.

Notes (Yours)

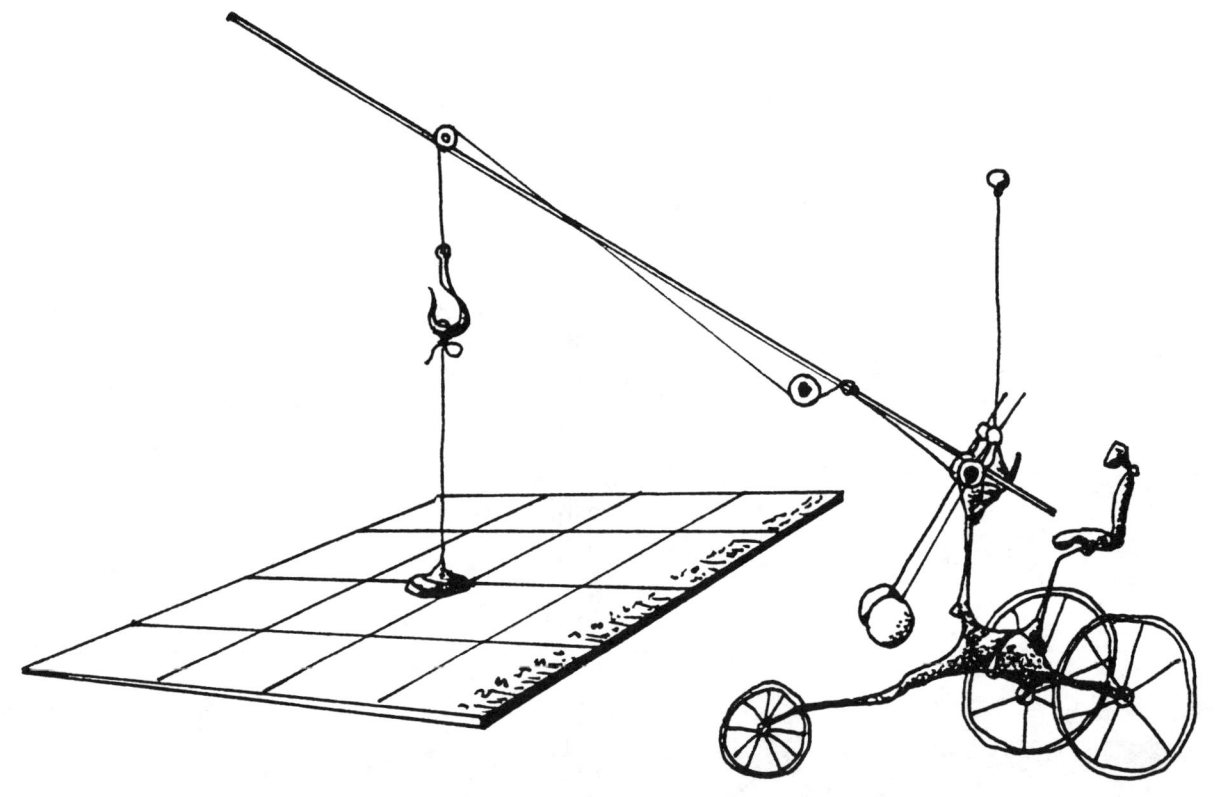

IV. Area and Weight

Section Notes

This section compounds the issues of component parts and wholes that were explored in Section I—with an additional idea that will eventually lead to density: the relationship of area to weight in objects of consistent thickness and material density. All of the problems are very similar; the twists in each are generally created to maintain interest and stimulate diversity of attack methods.

If you haven't gotten one yet, this is the point at which you can no longer make it without a good balance or a *very* patient class. Easier to obtain, but almost as important: **CARDBOARD**. Have lots of it on hand. Wood and sandpaper are also good, but cardboard is relatively uniform, easy to cut, ubiquitous, and cheap.

Problems 17 and 19 can be used as templates for many others. They are easy and quick to prepare and make good starting points. Problem 18 throws in triangles as parts of a square. Problem 22 can generate high drama.

17: Two Pieces of Wood

Problem: You have 2 pieces of wood, marked A and B. You also have a piece of cardboard, marked C, which is exactly twice the width of A, and twice the length of the B. Both pieces of wood were cut from the same board.

Determine the weight of both pieces of wood.

Details: You may weigh only one of the 3 objects (A, B, or C). You may not use other wood or measure the cardboard.

Margin of Error: 1 gram of actual weights.

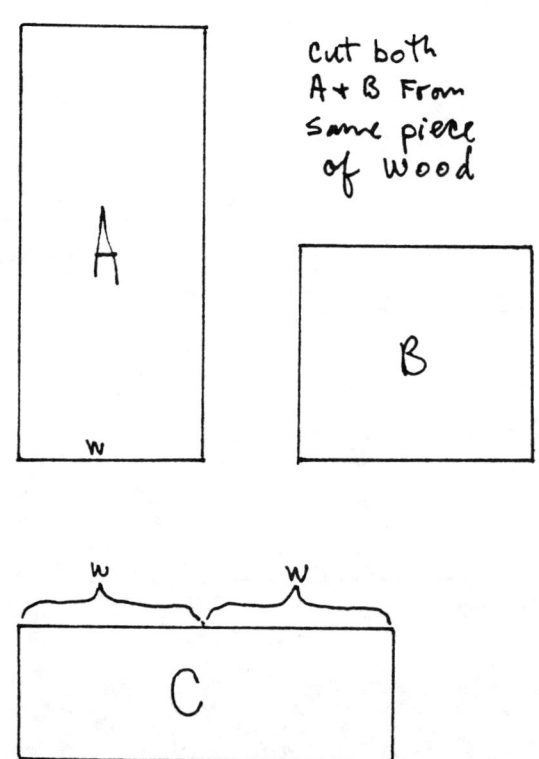

IV. Area and Weight

Teachers Notes:

This problem, like most of those in the Area and Weight section, explores the relationship between the weights and areas of objects of uniform thickness and density. The cardboard was thrown in to force thought about what information is significant in this situation.

As the problem seemingly relies on information about relative widths and lengths, be sure to cut the wood in a consistent way that takes into account the width of the saw cut.

Special Materials

- Square pieces of wood (uniform thickness) and cardboard (the cardboard must be cut to fit description). For an easy problem, cut 1 piece of wood to be twice the size of the other.
- Triple-beam balance

Spinoffs:

1. Give the weight of C as a percentage of A or B, and ask for the weight of another piece of cardboard (D), which can be measured but not weighed.
2. Throw in a triangle, circle, or regular polygon.

17: Two Pieces of Wood

18: Triangle and Rectangle with Bread

Problem: On the table, there's a large manila envelope containing seven coins (worth $0.82), taped together with 10" of Scotch tape. The envelope is taped to a large rectangle of cardboard. There's also a cardboard triangle attached to an identical envelope containing the same amount of tape—but no money. Find the weight of the cardboard triangle without touching it or the envelope attached.

Details: The triangle measures 4" x 8" x 8.9." You may not use other cardboard or envelopes, nor open the two envelopes. You may not separate any of the pieces from one another.

Margin of Error: 5% of triangle's actual weight

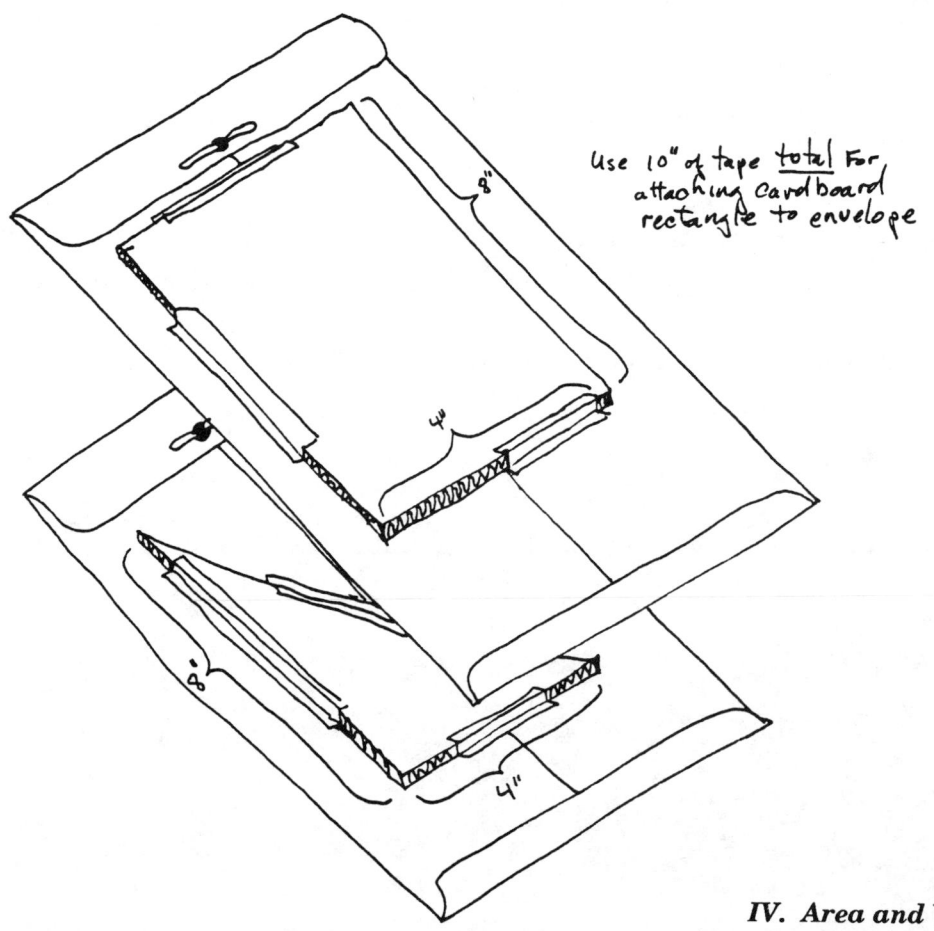

Use 10" of tape total for attaching cardboard rectangle to envelope

Teacher Notes:

This is a forest-for-the-trees special which really involves little beyond the fact that the triangle will be half of the weight of the rectangle (which should be 4" x 8"). There is a lot of component analysis that needs to be applied to the seeming complexity of the problem in order to arrive at the rectangle's weight, but it's no worse than anything in the Length, Number, and Weight sections of problems. Most groups do terribly on the first phase of the problem until someone starts drawing. It sometimes works wonders on the over-inflated egos of big talkers who are used to dominating groups.

Take care that you use the same amount of tape to attach the 2 envelopes to the cardboard pieces. Also, use heavy envelopes which don't allow the outlines of the coins to be seen through the paper (you could also tape the coins to a small piece of cardboard, but you'd then have to include this info in the problem description).

Special Materials:

- Two identical large manila envelopes
- 82 cents in change (7 coins)
- Scotch tape
- Cardboard
- Triple-beam balance

Spinoffs:

1. Use a rectangle that isn't twice the size of the triangle.

18: Triangle and Rectangle with Bread

19: Two for One

Problem: You have 2 pieces of cardboard. You can measure both, but you can't weigh the larger of the 2. Determine the weight of the larger piece without cutting either piece or using other cardboard.

Margin of Error:

Teacher Notes:

Cardboard is your friend. It's consistent, easily cut and available at a moment's notice anyplace in the United States. This is the kind of problem that you can put together in 5 minutes. It's simply another area-to-weight determination which exploits the fact that cardboard, as a relatively uniform material, directly varies its weight as a function of area. Almost all of the problems in this section are spinoffs of this idea.

For this reason, I won't generally bother with spinoffs after each problem in this section, but I would encourage you to use as many as needed until students become adept at determining area and weight per square unit, and more importantly, at using the information practically.

Special Materials:

- Square pieces of cardboard (uniform thickness)
- Triple-beam balance

20: Circular Reasoning

Problem: You can weigh, measure, eat, or do anything else with Fred, your piece of cardboard—as long as you return him in good shape. Your task: Find the size (area) of Fred's missing sister, Yvonne, a circle weighing _____ grams, who was cut from the same family of cardboard. And now there's no other cardboard in the world....

Margin of Error:

Teacher Notes:

Fred has seen other lives as an irregular shape whose outline featured protruding triangles and rectangles. Those versions required several separate area calculations to be added together to obtain the composite area. But in all versions, the problem still hinges on calculating weight per unit area.

Special Materials:

- Cardboard square (Fred) whose edges are of the exact size needed to contain a cardboard circle (Yvonne)

- Triple-beam balance

Spinoffs:

1. Determine the weight of Norbert, Yvonne's very square child, whose corners touched Yvonne's edge before he was cut out of her at birth.

21: Scratchy Snoods

Problem: You're given a circular piece of thick sandpaper that you may weigh and measure, but you may not damage or change it in any way.

Determine the weight of a ____" x ____" rectangular piece of the same kind of sandpaper that happens to be locked in the glove compartment of my car. It will get unlocked after you have come up with a terrifically accurate estimate of its weight. You get no other sandpaper to play with—and leave my car alone.

Margin of Error:

Teacher Notes:

As the basic problem should require no explanation after what has preceded it, consider some other issues.

1. Is everyone involved in all phases of solution?

2. Have you tried structuring problems in ways that promote dependence or competition? Why? Which works better? When? Why? Do the results vary with difficulty or grouping or the type of problem?

3. Can everyone in your class construct a strategy for solution? Some might not be able to carry out certain strategies because of math skill deficits, but everyone should be able to describe what needs to be done.

4. Are the skills and concepts that are explored in one kind of problem being retained and transferred to others?

5. Is everyone capable of recognizing absurd solutions—solutions that just aren't reasonable?

6. How reasonable are the margins of error proposed by your students?

7. Is your class approaching a point where you could set a problem's instructions and materials out on a table and leave the classroom for 2 hours? (Few teaching situations would allow this or make it reasonable to try, but it's a valuable mental experiment and evaluative check.)

Special Materials:

- Rectangular and circular pieces of <u>very</u> coarse, heavy sandpaper
- Triple-beam balance

22: Out of Whack

Problem: In the homemade balance in front of you are 3 pieces of sandpaper, all cut from the same brand and thickness. A circle ___ cm. across and a ___ cm. x ___ cm. rectangle are in one bucket of the balance. In the other bucket, there's a square piece of sandpaper which is ___ cm. long on each side.

You'll be given *one* sheet of the sandpaper. Your job is to cut one piece out of it which, when put into one of the buckets, will balance the whole shebang exactly. You cannot take out any of the pieces, *and you only get one shot* (no adding little pieces, one at a time).

Margin of Error: The pointer should be less than 1/8" away from the center line.

Teacher Notes:

This problem is one that might be especially important to try before you use it. Unless you're very handy, get a hold of a balance that works—from someone who teaches first or second grade. You can make a balance, but unless the swing of the arm is *very* smooth, it won't work well enough to save you from lynching by students who, after an hour of careful work on the problem, then suspect and angrily prove that your balance doesn't work (this is not an imaginary scenario—and it's not pretty). The problem can also be done with a triple-beam balance, but it loses the visual impact.

When this works, it's beautiful. The lowering of the exactly cut and sweated over piece of sandpaper into the bucket never fails to silence the room. A slowing swing down and a stop dead center can actually produce applause.

Special Materials:

- A balance—homemade or not—large enough to hold 3 pieces of sandpaper cut into a square, rectangle, and circle of about 16 square inches each. It's easy to modify a playschool balance, but test it yourself.

- Very heavy sandpaper cut into a circle, square, and rectangle.

- A whole sheet of the same sandpaper

Spinoffs:

1. Use water and coins in one bucket, and water in the other. Charge your students with the task of adding the correct number of water drops (from a pipette or eyedropper) to balance the apparatus.

2. Add coins to equalize 2 unequal containers of water.

23: Planely Shaped

Problem: On the table, there is one pile made of 7 loose pieces of sandpaper, cut into different shapes, and another pile of sandpaper disks that are taped together with 60 cm. of tape. *You may weigh only 1 of the 7 shapes.* You may not weigh the disks nor use any other sandpaper.

Determine the weight of *each* loose piece of sandpaper. Don't rub, bend or change any of the shapes, since that may change its weight (sand rubs off the sandpaper), thus ruining your chances for an accurate answer.

Margin of Error: 4% of actual weight of each piece.

Teacher Notes:

A straightforward problem complicated only by the number of calculations involved, this is a good one for delegating answers and encouraging checking and communication. And watch which object is chosen to weigh. This will indicate whether or not any or all of the group members are thinking strategically.

Special Materials:

- 5-10 identical heavy sandpaper disks
- 7 assorted shapes cut from the same weight sandpaper
- Triple-beam balance
- Masking tape

Notes (Yours)

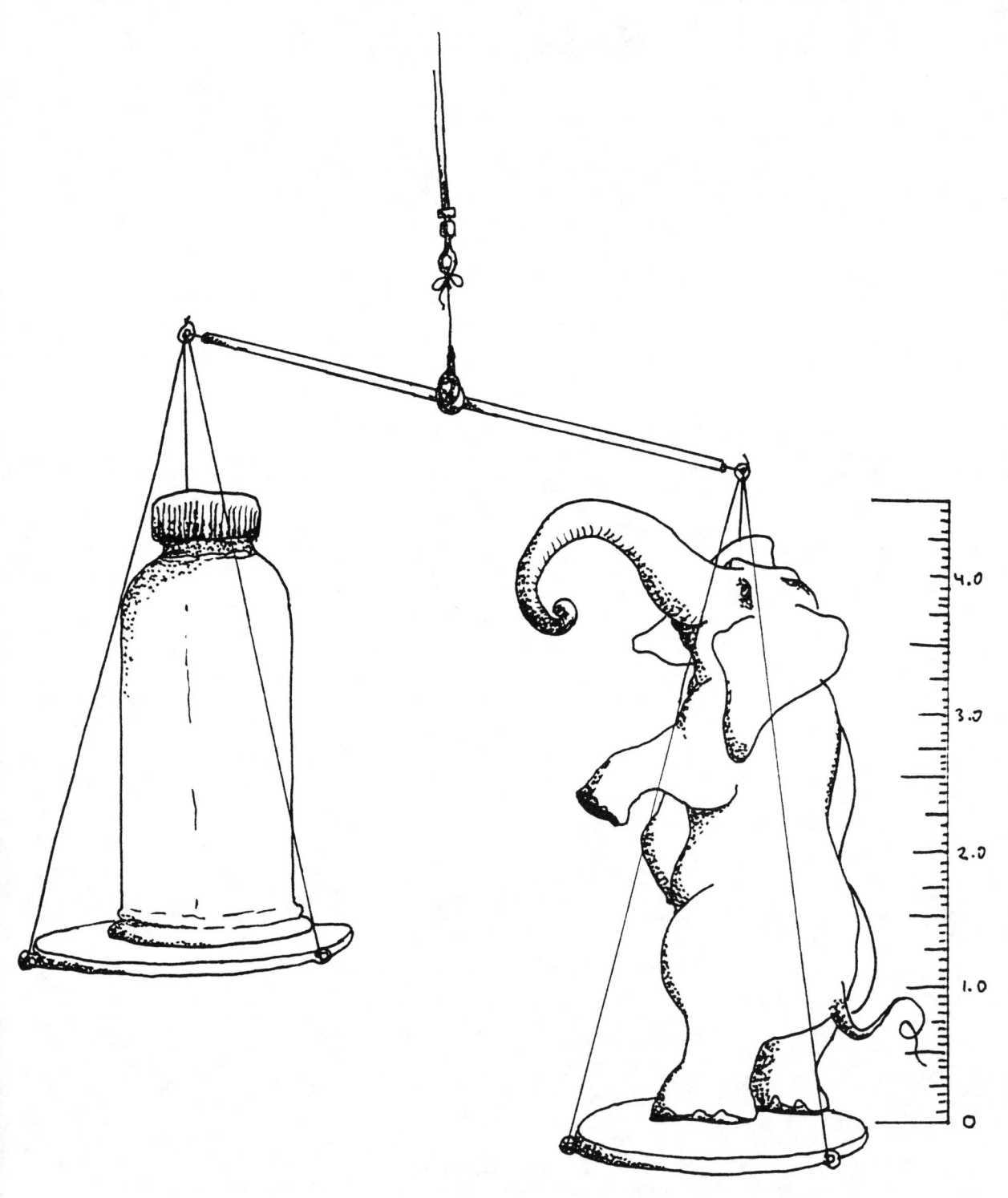

V. Density, Weight and Volume

Section Notes

In my experience, these problems were the ones that finally wove together the great tangle of investigative threads that had been worked on in other problems. Many students finally discovered here that known aspects of reality were allies in their quests (imposed by me) to understand other features of it. It was here that they finally learned to "cheat:" instead of measuring a volume through complicated formulae and measurements, they could simply fill it with something weighable and then translate that weight into volume.

While the whole inquiry-driven approach relies on students locating their own routes to understanding, more of these routes will be available if students have some experience with liquid measurement techniques and are comfortable with balances, pipettes, and other paraphernalia before they hit this kind of problem. Obviously, it's easier to understand the concept of density with a good handle on weight and volume than without one. But this is not to say that your particular group should not attempt such problems before they have been checked off on the appropriate skills (after all, you can't be sure what those skills are in every case.) It does mean, however, that you should assess the group level of competence with the central concepts that are <u>likely</u> to be used—and balance that assessment against the group's tenacity and ability to tolerate frustration and failure.

All of the problems here revolve around using density to determine either volume from weight, or weight from volume. Determining density is not an endpoint. Rather, it is attacked through problems that hinge upon it as the <u>tool</u> needed to determine other things. The satisfaction that I derived from watching students attempt these problems is probably located in this fact. It is a rare and precious moment in the life of a teacher when a concept is learned from the gitgo as something *needed* rather than something dictated.

There is little to think about here concerning the order of presentation except that the tube problems (29 and 30) are a little more difficult for students to visualize than those involving more "normal" shapes. Doodah #2 is a little different from the others in that it generally encourages a lot of volume calculation. It is closer than the others to a typical math or science problem in that it generally builds one concept from others, in a predictable sequence.

24: Doodah #2

Problem: Calculate the exact weight of either Doodah (the 5-piece Deluxe model or the 2-piece Economy Doodah)—*without weighing it.*

Details: You may weigh the *other* Doodah *once.* You may measure both in any other way(s) that you wish. You can use water, measuring devices, clay, paper—anything at all—as long as you do not actually weigh the Mystery Doodah.

Treat these fine-quality Doodahs with care. Although they are made of the highest grade scrap wood and Elmer's Glue, they may lose weight and suffer reduced performance if dropped or nicked.

The wages of Doodah damage are death.

Margin of Error:

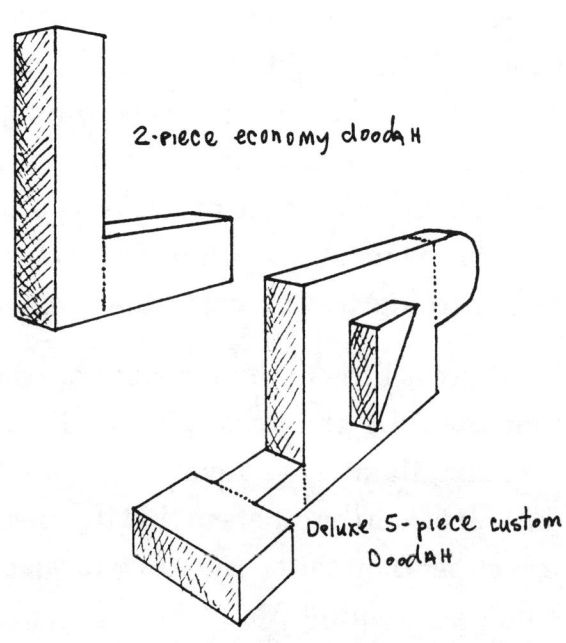

96   V. *Density, Weight and Volume*

Teacher Notes:

The elaborateness of the Doodahs is up to you and your estimation of your group's readiness to handle irregular shapes etc. In most cases, the 2-piece model is simply a combination of rectangles, although I have included curves or triangles in one or both Doodahs when I've wanted to force understanding of area calculations for these shapes.

Generally, the simpler the problem, the more difficult your construction process. Use simple shapes—maybe with whole-number dimensions—for groups that are not ready for irregular shapes requiring expert estimation and many calculations. This is not always easy to do if your own tools and methods aren't precise. On the other hand, for a highly skilled group looking for a challenge, your sloppiness is their gain: Sawdust in the glue, chunks and nicks out of the wood, and other irregularities, all add to the richness of the problem (as long as the margin of error is demanding enough).

Special Materials:

- 1" to 3" pieces of scrap wood, all of the same density. It's best to use pieces cut from one board, but be careful—even some boards are composites whose density varies. Also, avoid knots in the wood.
- Elmer's glue
- Triple-beam balance

25: Shampoo Bottle

Problem: The shampoo bottle in front of you is partially filled with water. You may not open or damage it in any way. Feel free to have a good time with the extra bottle cap that is also in front of you.

Predict the weight of the shampoo bottle when it's empty and dry. Naturally, you may use anything or anyone to solve the problem as long as you don't violate the rules laid out or use another identical shampoo bottle.

Margin of Error:

Teacher Notes:

Although the concept here is not particularly difficult, this particular problem requires either a calculation of a cylinder's volume, or some other strategy which recreates the volume of the liquid. I have seen groups find the formula (sometimes even the right one) in reference books. I have also had groups derive cylindrical volume as a percentage of a square-bottomed 3-d rectangle of the same height. Still others have attacked the idea by displacing water with the bottle and trying to guess how much to subtract for the minor difference between the inside and outside of the submerged portion of the bottle.

In general, the consideration of volume as it relates to liquids and the shapes they *fill* (rather than rigidly *define*, as is the case for solid materials like wood and cardboard) is often a new way of looking at volume for students. Eventually, you want to bring them to the concept of volume as a way of looking at space, rather than a special-case formula like H×W×L.

So there's more here than meets the eye. For some groups, the introduction of liquid measurement into the problems is the revolutionary event that ties many things together. Liquids have the convenient property of exactly filling (and defining) space. In many cases, when students add this to an understanding that they can now essentially measure weight with volume (and vice versa), they win a new and more powerful understanding of volume, weight, and density.

Also, the introduction of liquid into problems generally means some work on student technique. As things become more complex and/or exacting, water temperature, stray drops, etc. will become increasingly important matters for them to consider.

Special Materials:

- Shampoo bottle of regular shape with cap (Flex shampoo types are great, with an almost perfect cylindrical shape)
- Extra bottle cap—identical to the shampoo bottle cap
- Triple-beam balance
- Pipettes

Spinoffs:

1. Put a few items in the bottle (and leave duplicates on the table.)
2. Use a different liquid.

26: Boxawaddah

Problem: We wont be in the class room at all until later in the morning. we expeckt you to work on this problem without us, of corse everbody should be involve'd.

In order to suceed you not only have to solve the problem but correct the instruction's so that their is to mistakes or lest. It will be up to you to decide how to devide up your time and do these to thing's. We don't expect no complaints from no other staff about noise or students from this class wanderin around the hallways

Your given a plastic box, your job is to figure out were 400 grams of water will rise to when its poured into the box.

Details: You can't put anything at all in the box when you think you no were the water will rise to, you have to draw a line on the inside of the box to show wher the water line will be. You can't put any water or liquid in the box.

Margin of Error: Since were leaving you on your own and wont be around to mess thing's up, youll need to be within 1/4" of the actual waterline to suceed.

Teacher Notes:

Although the messed-up instructions are a spinoff suggested earlier (and can be used at any time), I thought it might help to include one set. I employed this wrinkle on a day when we wanted to promote maximum involvement over a long unsupervised period of time. The mistakes reflect the usual problem areas in

V. Density, Weight and Volume

spelling and grammar. Although most situations won't allow your actual absence, I left in the missing-teacher element to indicate the aim: student direction of the entire process—multiple responsibilities, strategy, time-use, group involvement, cooperation, accuracy, and analysis. The group must work as adults, assuming complete responsibility for generating an acceptable result in an acceptable way.

The problem itself is a simple determination of straight-sided volume and liquid density. Judge the skill of the group when selecting the margin of error and container size. Check your box for water-tightness before presenting the problem.

Special Materials:

- Plastic (or other watertight) box with dimensions of about 3" x 5" x 4". Avoid rounded edges and boxes with decorative or manufacturing features such as depressions in the bottom. Avoid boxes too large to show much rise in water level with 400 grams of water or boxes so narrow and tall that even a few drops will change the level drastically.

- Pipettes

- Triple-beam balance

Spinoffs:

1. Use a round container (bottle or can).

2. Add a little drama by asking the students to compete in putting their water line measurements on the outside of the (opaque) container. After the water is poured in, cover the top so no one can see where the actual water level is and start drilling holes (with a *non-electric* drill, thank you very much) at each mark—highest first. The winner is whoever manages the lowest mark without a leak (remove your lunch from the danger zone).

3. Same as spinoff #2, but leave your lunch near the can.

4. Same as spinoff #3, but leave someone else's lunch near the can.

27: Heavy Can

Problem: Predict exactly what a can will weigh when filled with water (up to the bottom of the piece of tape inside the can.) You can do anything you need to in order to make your prediction except put water in the can (or any other can of the exact same bottom size.)

Details: As usual, we'll try to obtain whatever equipment you need in order to solve the problem. Feel free to get help from anyone you think appropriate.

For this particular problem, every person in the class will have to come up with his or her own estimate. If they're all the same, that's fine, but each of you will have to show one of us how you arrived at your estimate. It's up to you whether or not you want to work alone, as a whole group, or in some other combination.

Margin of Error: 5% of the actual weight of the can when filled up with water. Only those with estimates within the required margin of error will qualify for the Mystery Prize.

Teacher Notes:

Don't use a can that will weigh more than the capacity of your balance (usually about 500 g.) when filled with water—unless you want to extend the activity to include balance construction.

The stipulation of separate estimates is an indication of problems with passive non-participants. Prizes are another indicator of trouble—though they're not a bad idea to foster involvement early in the year. Generally, though, if you consistently need prizes or threats to foster involvement in this process, something is not right in Denmark (do not assume for a moment, however, that I ever developed my problems and group interaction to the point that I could consistently forget these philosophically "incorrect" tools. In real classrooms that exist outside of pedagogical theory textbooks, the level of student involvement and inner motivation doesn't hit 100% very often).

Special Materials:

- 1 Can, without many ridges, depressions, or other irregularities (soup and vegetable cans work well)
- Pipettes
- Triple-beam balance
- Masking Tape

Spinoffs:

1. Check for success with a student-weighing apparatus.
2. Stipulate that students must find or create an object that will weigh the same as the water-filled can. No liquids allowed. No composites made of more than 5 pieces.

28: Pepsi Generation

Problem: You have 3 Pepsi cans, each carefully and thoroughly rinsed and dried. One of the cans is empty and weighs exactly _____ g. The second is partially filled with water and weighs _____ g. The third is full and weighs _____ g.

You must mark the level to which the water will rise if I pour both cans into the other container that you are given. You may not put anything inside of that container except your mark. You may not move or lift any of the Pepsi cans.

Margin of Error:

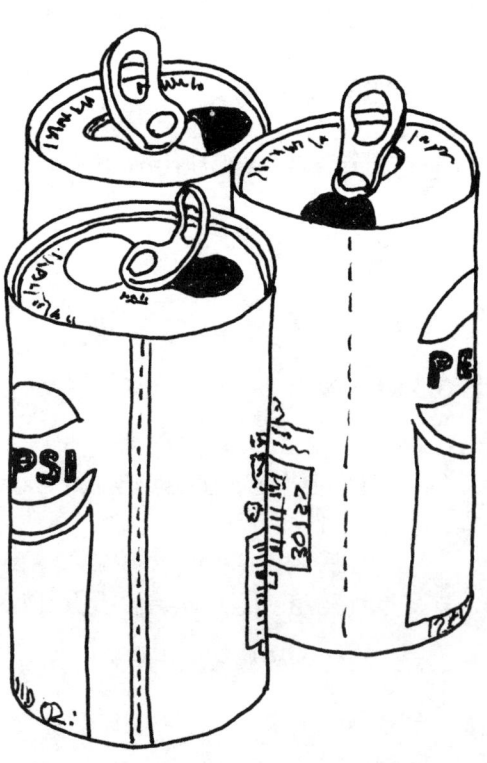

Teacher Notes:

This is a good one for promoting cooperative effort because it suggests separate determinations which are combined to produce a single answer. The simple part of the problem is to determine the weight of the water in each can before the weights are translated into volumes. The more difficult phase is to equate volume with water level in the container, a task which can be made harder or easier by the shape of the container.

Special Materials:

- Three identical cans (I used Pepsi cans only because I needed them in a hurry), one empty, one full of water, and one containing another amount of water. Each needs to be carefully weighed. It's a good idea to draw circles around each can on the table and then allow no movement of the cans from the circles.

- Fourth container, large enough to hold all of the water in the three cans.

- Pipettes

- Triple-beam balance

Spinoffs:

1. Use an irregularly shaped container.

2. Use a container which won't hold all of the water and ask for the water level of the remaining unpoured water in one of the 2 cans.

29: Radically Tubular, Fersure

Problem: Dudes, check out the sealed plastic tube, marked near one end. Also, like, look at the smaller piece of tubing that was cut from the larger one before it was sealed.

Estimate, fersure, how many milliliters of water it will take to fill the tube from the bottom to the mark.

Details: We'll determine the accuracy of your estimate by cutting the tube and pouring in the water that you give me. Neither tube can be cut or changed in any way until your estimate is submitted to The Committee for the Promotion of Accurate Tubular Volume Determination.

Margin of Error:

Teacher Notes:

This is similar to other cylindrical volume problems, but requires that students realize that a tube is just a squiggled up cylinder with a narrow diameter. Flexible clear plastic hose is available at hardware stores. The problem is somehow most compelling if you seal the ends by heating them and squeezing with a clamp or pliers. This is dramatic—we can't find out the answer without cutting the tube. Unfortunately, sealing the tubes by pinching the ends distorts the cylindrical shape at both seals, so don't use this method unless the overall volume is large enough to minimize the distortion's impact (or unless your group is sophisticated enough to account for the distortion). I've also used PVC tubing with caps and a variety of stoppers and corks in various types of hosing with some success. Any combination that doesn't leak and is close to transparent will work. Write the publisher if you find the perfect material and sealing method.

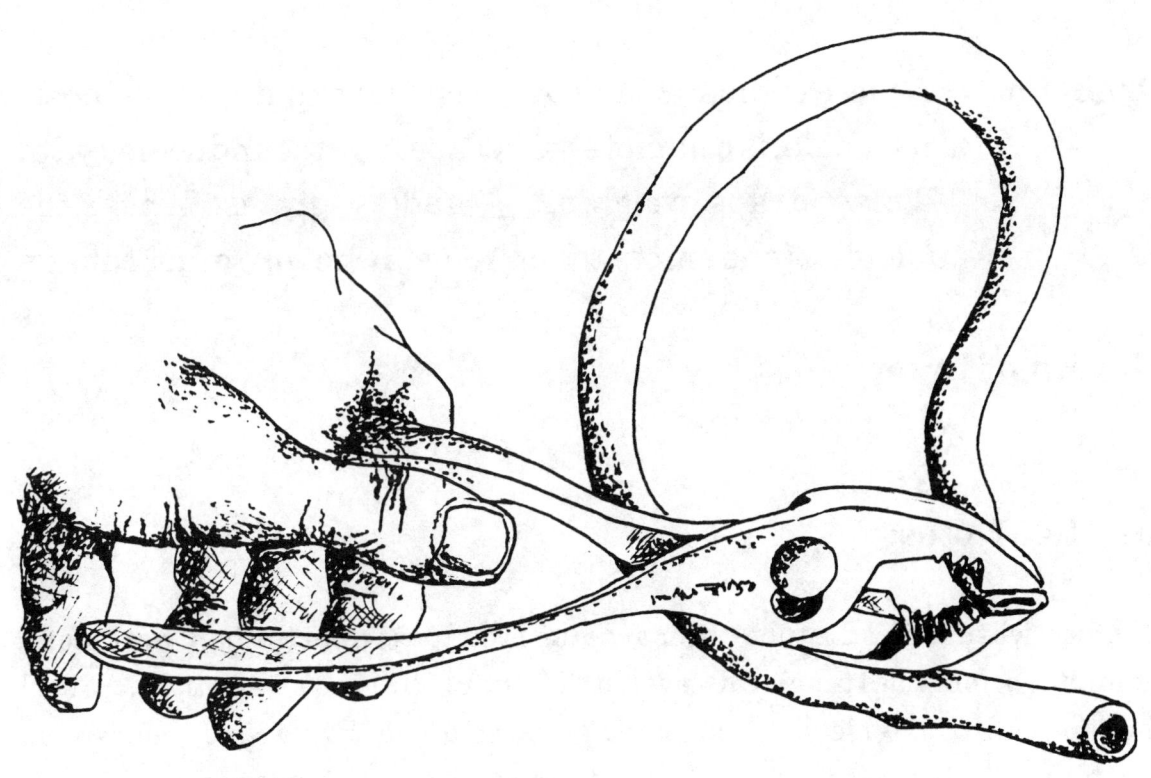

Special Materials:

- 2' to 10' of transparent plastic flexible tubing, one large piece and one small one (6" or less). Seal the large piece at both ends by melting them shut with an iron or heated screw driver blade.

- Pipettes

- Triple-beam balance

Spinoffs:

1. Place BB's or other regular space-consumers in the sealed tube.

30: Tubesoak

Problem: A piece of plastic tubing, ___ cm. long and ___ cm. across its inside, is completely filled with water and sealed with 2 plastic caps, weighing ___ and ___ grams. What's the weight of the empty tube? You may not use other tubing.

Margin of Error: 5%

Teacher Notes:

Once, when filling the tube (after arriving breathless from the hardware store, 3 minutes before class time), I discovered that the caps weren't watertight. So seal the caps with a watersealing compound/glue *and allow drying time*—unless you relish the idea of creating a replacement project during attendance.

Special Materials:

- Rigid tubing (PVC or other), of about 1" diameter and less than 2' in length, filled with water and sealed (watertight—with caps at both ends). Locate caps which flatly cover the tube ends—nothing puffy.
- Pipettes
- Triple-beam balance

Spinoffs:

1. Students mark a predicted waterline on a container into which the water is poured from the tube during final testing.

Notes (Yours)

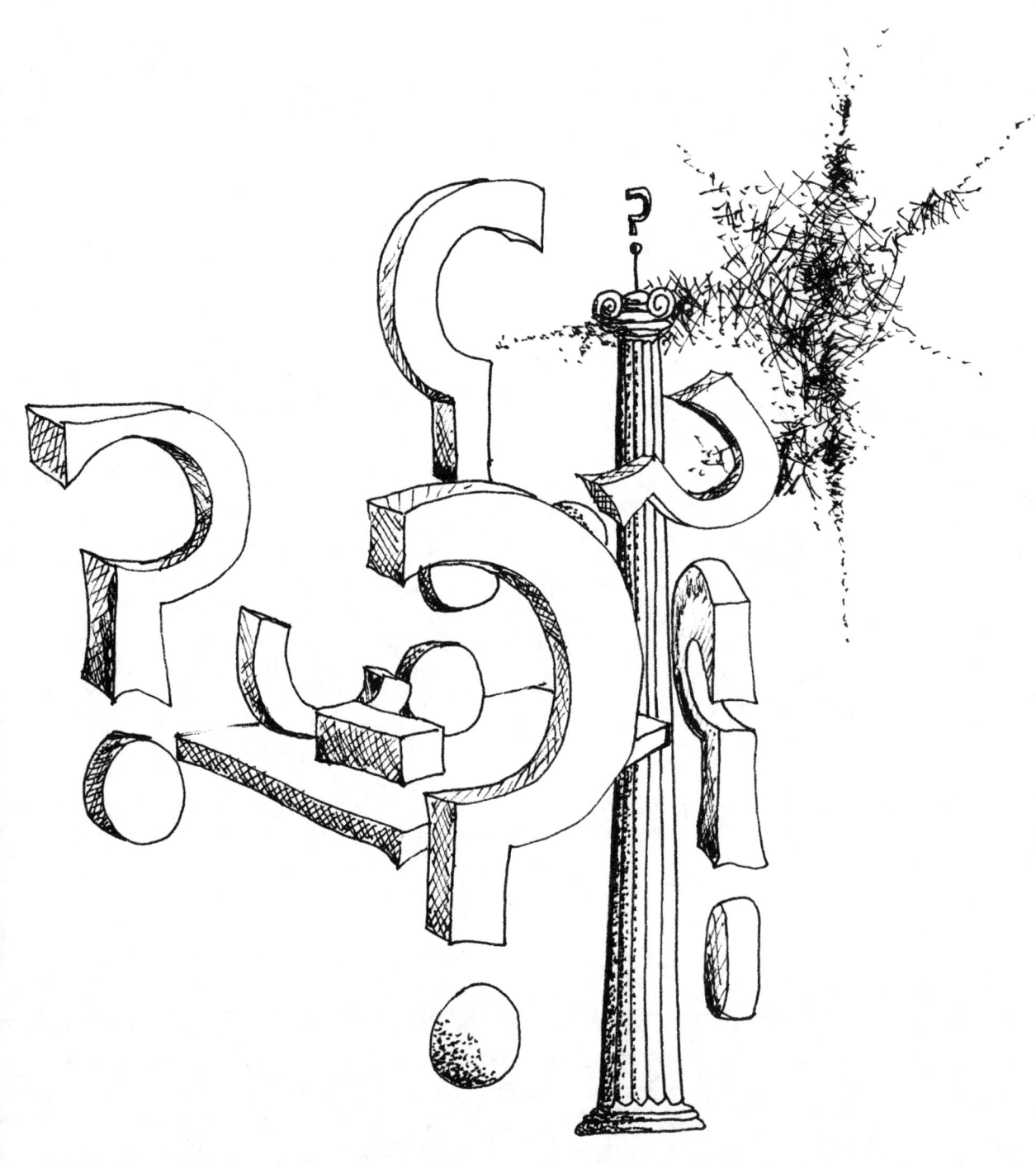

VI. Density and Identity

Section Notes

This section contains three difficult problems (difficult both to present and to solve): Density is used to identify different "hidden" materials. There are only three problems in this section because I never brought a group to this point much before the year ended. Also, in looking for liquids and materials of varying densities that were significant but not otherwise problematic (corrosive, expensive, difficult to handle and shape, or toxic), I was entering the realm of supply-house science, a place I had generally avoided. I found myself wishing for things not found at the hardware store. I could have used, but never found, for instance, an easily decipherable chart of specific gravities. Materials of different but similar densities demanded a precision in measurement of weight that was often beyond that of our triple-beam balances. I ran into problems of concentration and purity —materials and compounds available in everyday life are generally mixtures and alloys other things.

Your situation may not constrained by any or all of these factors. In spite of my limited experience and success with this kind of problem, it offers something worth a lot more work—it demonstrates a *practical* utility of density as an identifier of materials. I hope that some users of this book will go beyond these first steps and write to me. A second edition should be fatter here.

31: Three Bottles

Problem: You get three bottles, labelled 1, 2, and 3 (clever, huh?). Their dry (empty) weights are:

#1: _____ grams
#2: _____ grams
#3: _____ grams

Bottle #1 is empty, but each of the others contains 100 milliliters of liquid. Determine which of the full bottles contains water and which (if either) contains something else. *You must offer a reasoning behind your determination* ("I guessed" is not good enough). You may not open either for any reason. You may use bottle #1 however you wish—as long as it remains empty. You may also use any other resources that you feel would be helpful (feel free to call Mom, if it's a local call).

Margin of Error: If you're really good, you'll be able to figure out exactly what's in each bottle.

Teacher Notes:

Use opaque bottles that seal tightly and don't allow any odor to escape. You want the determination to be made on the basis of density, not smell, color, or viscosity. If you think your class might be sophisticated enough to ferret out the concept and existence of specific gravity lists, head for your high school chemistry department and see what liquid they can give you that isn't dangerous but is listed in the tables your students might lay hold of. A good selection is something different enough from water that a weight discrepancy will be measurable on your equipment, but not so different that you can feel the difference without a scale.

If you get the idea from this description that it isn't so easy to locate such a liquid, you are painfully correct. Although I eventually found just what I was looking for, the process was so educational that you shouldn't be deprived of it.

In the case that none of this seems likely, all you need is a liquid with a different density than water. You can make suspensions of sand, for instance, that will work fine, or experiment with non-toxic liquids and mixtures used in day-to-day life. It's nice if you can locate bottles that have exactly the same weight, but I've never managed to do this. Since the difference in liquid densities is usually a relatively small one, a 1 or 2 gram discrepancy in bottle weights can be very significant.

Special Materials:

- 3 opaque, identical 100cc bottles that seal tightly enough so that no odor escapes—preweighed dry, before being filled
- 100 cc's each of water and the Mystery Liquid
- Pipettes
- Triple-beam balance

Spinoffs:

1. Ask groups to create specific gravity lists for common liquids.
2. Determine whether adding salt or sugar to water changes its density.
3. Make a guess about the relative densities of oil, vinegar, and water based on a container holding 50 ml. of each. Test the theory.

32: Prospecting

Problem: There are three identical bottles in front of you. Each is filled with the volume of liquid that will fill a fourth container to a level of exactly ___ cm. above its bottom. This fourth container is made of glass, is straight-sided and is ___ cm. in diameter. It weighed ___ grams before being partially filled with salad oil.

Without opening any of the bottles or the glass container in front of you, determine whether any or all of the bottles contain oil, water, or something else. You may use other tools/supplies in your work—*except* for bottles and containers of the same size as those in the problem.

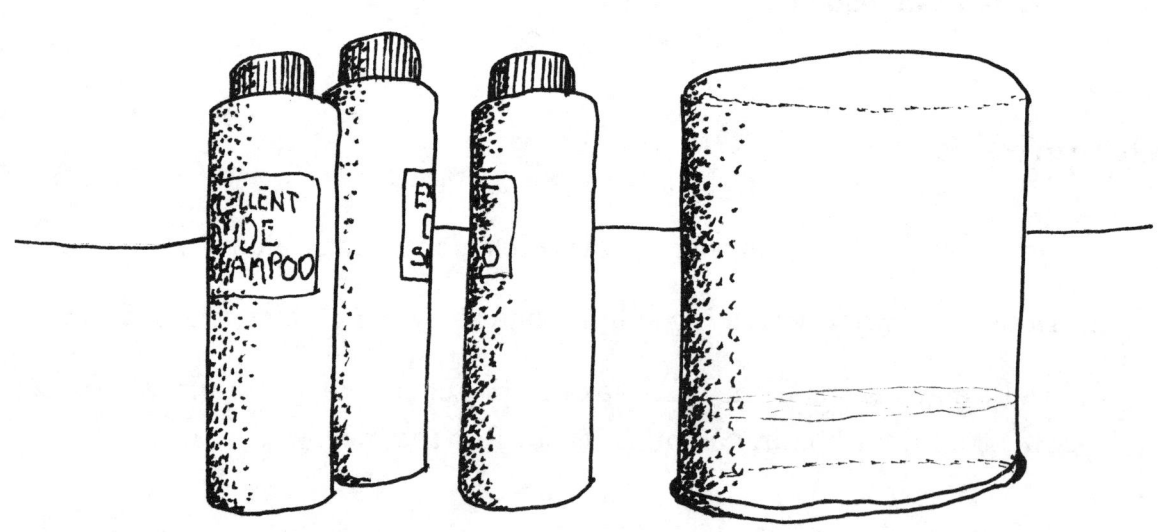

VI. Density and Identity

Teacher Notes:

If you haven't already discovered this the hard way in another problem, look for bottles and containers with flat, featureless bottoms. Also, the narrower the diameter of the container, the more accurate are volume determinations made on the basis of waterline.

This problem contains a lot of pieces and can require quite a bit of time. Students need to be very clear on the difference between volume and weight to do it. This may seem to be an obvious difference, but when dealing with water, the two seem to be the same (1 ml. of water = approx. 1 gram) to students who ignore units and just "do the numbers."

Special Materials:

- 3 opaque, identical 100cc bottles that seal tightly enough so that no odor escapes.
- One straight-sided glass container with a 200-400 cc capacity
- Salad Oil, Water, and Mystery Liquid
- Pipettes
- Triple-beam balance

Spinoffs:

1. Predict the weight of all of the liquid added together and test the prediction.
2. Predict the volume of all of the liquid added together and test the prediction.

33: Hollow Box

Problem: On the table are 5 identically-sized blocks of wood (all of the same type of wood). On the shelf is a triple-beam balance holding an identical set of 5 blocks, but with a ____ cm. x ____ cm. square cut out of the middle three, to form a box. The balance is set at exactly the current weight of the box and its contents. You can't see those contents unless you remove the top or bottom piece—but (surprise!) you're not allowed even to touch the thing.

What *three* identical objects are in the box?

Details: These objects are very common. In fact, one or more objects of the same type are in sight of everyone in the room. Once you have decided what's in the box, arrange evidence that will prove that you could be right.

Teacher Notes:

The weight of the box involves a density calculation, but the determination of what's in it is simply a location of a visible object that is 1/3 of the additional weight in the box. Pennies, electrical outlet covers, and screws are good choices.

The elaborate description of the box can be simplified, depending on your needs and luck in locating a suitable pre-assembled box. "Suitable" here means "with a simple rectangular cavity and of a material of consistent density *and* available for placing on the table." Those aspects are crucial: Students must be able to assume that the material they're given and that of the box are identical; and a complex cavity is too hard to describe (although you could refocus the problem by using a complex drawing, thus making the box's weight noxiously difficult to figure).

As written, this problem requires two balances—one for the box, and one for students to work with. You could get by with one balance and simply give the weight of the box and contents, but this would destroy a little of the visual drama.

Special Materials:

- 10 blocks of wood—all of the same type and density—three with holes cut as shown in the drawing below and formed into a box
- 4 identical objects—three of them placed inside the 5-block box on the balance and one normally visible in the classroom.
- 2 Triple-beam balances

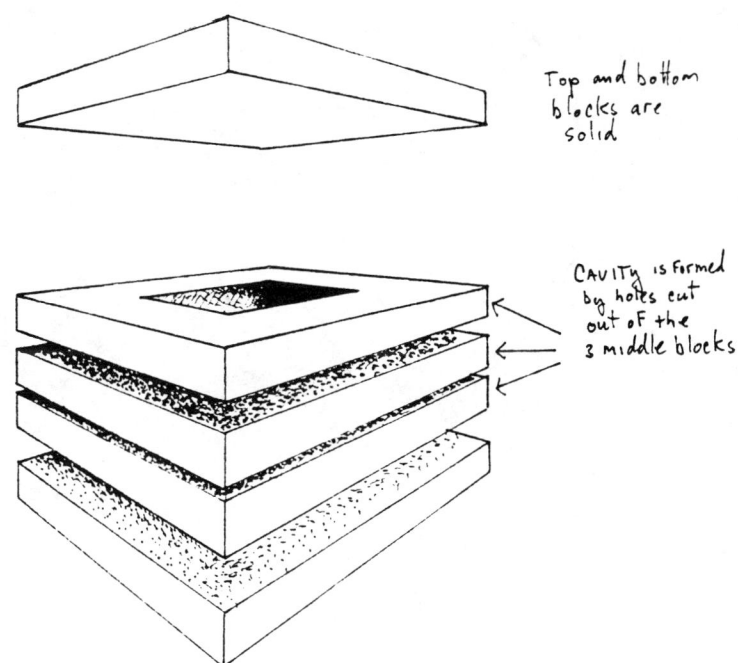

Spinoffs:

1. Say nothing about the size of the cavity. Explain what's in the box and ask students to predict the size of the cavity (you must supply duplicate objects).

2. With a really well-crafted box, ask for a prediction of the its weight if the cavity is filled with (A) water plus the 3 objects, and (B) water only.

3. Same as spinoff #2 except ask for the volume of water which will fill the cavity with and without the objects inside.

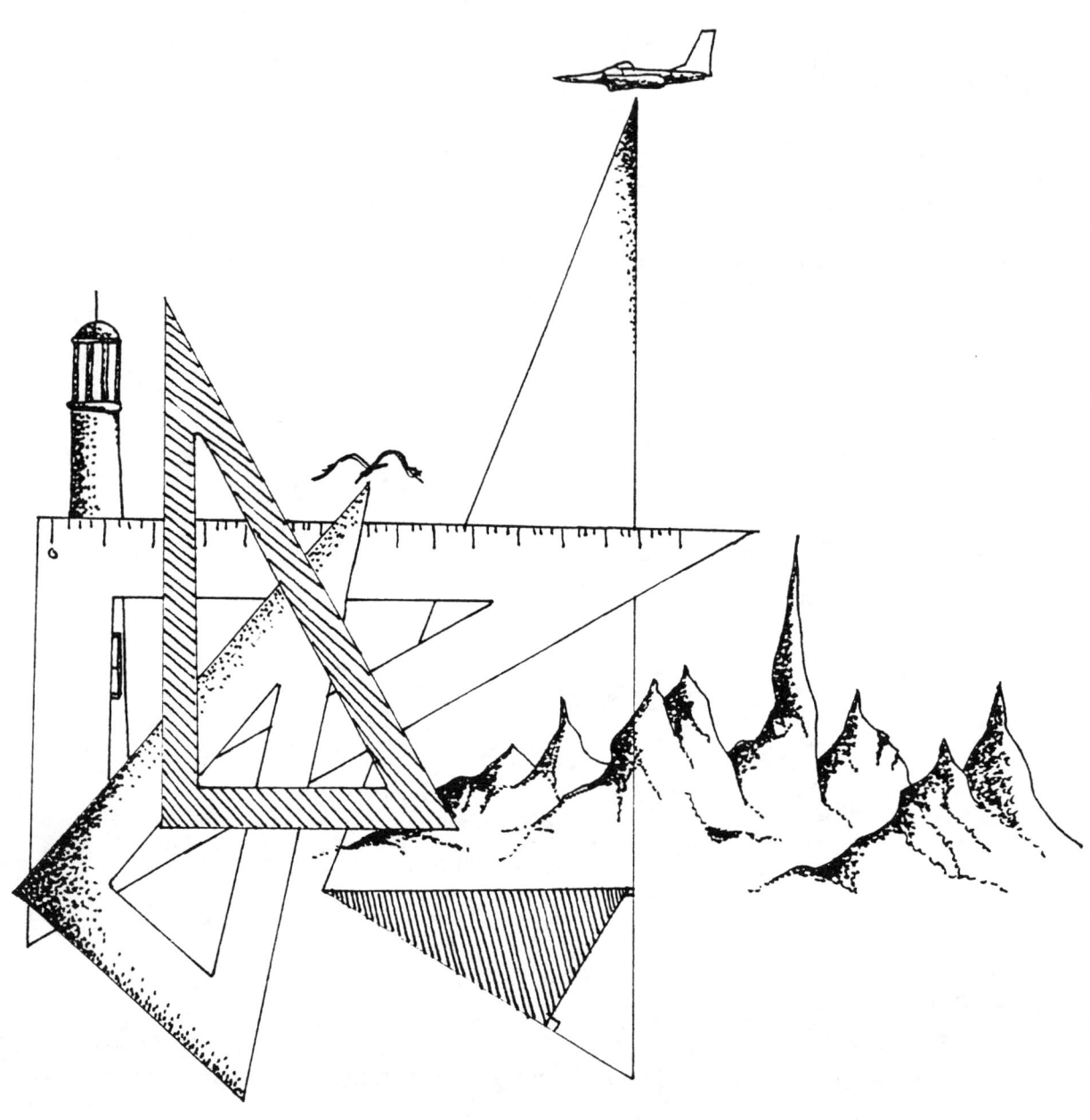

VII. Triangulation

Section Notes

This is another short section that seems rich in unexplored possibilities. Although *I* see triangulation as a fascinating tool, both of these (and the many other problems that I created to explore the concept) were easily thwarted by students who solved them in other ways, none of which seemed to employ triangles.

My ideas for future problems all exploit a larger scale. In this way, I hope to create situations in which triangulation is the only practical way to determine large distances that can't be directly measured. As of yet, however, I haven't developed problems that operate on such a scale but are still easily testable and verifiable. Rockets with primitive altimeters of some sort are an interesting idea, but feature a larger-than-comfortable technical and equipment-dependent element—and questionable accuracy. I'm also considering high bridges.

The basic problem lies in the fact that if I have to develop some other way to verify triangulated student results, there is no reason to assume that students will not devise these same (or other) methods instead of using triangles.

The tenacity with which students have resisted triangles in favor of other solutions leads me to think that the method presents some difficulties which I don't yet fully understand. Perhaps they are afraid of angles. Maybe the idea of modeling a solution (turning the world into a scaled drawing featuring an imagined triangle) is just not credible for some students. In any case, the issue deserves more time and effort.

34: Hose Tower

Problem: Estimate the height of the white object on the hose tower while remaining on the ground.

Details: You may do anything that doesn't involve physically leaving ground level or extending your height with ladders, poles, sticks, etc. Once you explain your estimate, we will determine the actual height of the object by attaching a pole or string between it and the ground directly below it, then measuring the string or pole with a 50' tape measure.

Although you may enlist the aid of other people, they cannot help you unless they stay at ground level also.

Margin of Error:

Teacher Notes:

Of course, your school may not feature a hose tower with a white object high above the ground—but you'll find something. The problem is particularly intriguing if the object is truly inaccessible, yet seen every day.

Although this section is labelled triangulation—and in spite of my doing everything I could think of to push kids toward the concept—they found other ways to solve the problems.

Special Materials:

- Easily discernible mark or object high enough up a building so as not to be easily reached without wings
- Snow rake or extendable pole
- String
- Lots of tape measures, rulers, yardsticks
- 50' foot tape measure
- Protractor or materials to build a tool to determine and/or record angles
- Graph paper

Spinoffs:

1. Rather than *you* measuring to verify the predictions, ask the students to somehow accurately measure the height of the object—without restrictions.

2. Call in an engineer or contractor to explain how they would go about making the same determination (don't bother if it's an easy ladder shot).

3. Assign a group of students the task of locating and bringing in a professional who accurately measures heights that can't be directly measured (surveyor, pilot, cartographer, air controller, etc.).

4. Predict the amount of time it will take for an object to fall from the mark to the ground.

5. Drop a rock from a high bridge and ask students to predict the height of the bridge (measured with kite string to verify). It's probably a good idea to avoid bridges over roads, etc., but there are many safe ones over river banks.

35: Telephone Pole

Problem: The telephone pole directly in front of the building is anchored by a cable that attaches about halfway up the pole. At what height does the cable attach to the pole? The distance from the base of the pole to the anchor point where the cable attaches to the ground is 12' 9".

Details: You must solve this without getting any closer than 10 feet to the pole, and you'll have only a 5-minute observation period to get even that close. At all other times, you'll be no closer than the classroom window.

Margin of Error: No more than 4%. That's 4 inches off for every 100 inches of actual height. The height will be determined by a Fearless Student, who will climb the pole and drop a string from the attachment point to the ground.

Teacher Notes:

Again, you may have to find an analogous situation. All you need is a tall object with a good oblique line attached. Ham radio antennas come to mind, but almost anything steadied by taut guy wires will serve admirably. A roof peak works, too.

As I said, although students enjoyed these problems, they were too good (for my taste) at solving them without triangles. Calling city architects for blue print specs and other methods showed exactly the kind of initiative and inventiveness that I had hoped to build with this approach, but I really wanted my students to understand the usefulness of the triangle in finding distant position and measurement. To satisfy my curricularly straight-jacketed mind, I even cheated: During the observation period, I lay on my stomach next to the wire and made mysterious arm movements with protractors and pieces of wood which I laid along the angle of the wire. Before that—still in the classroom—as students strategized and schemed, I feverishly drew triangles on little scraps of paper with 12' 9" labelled along the base and question marks up the altitude (labelled "T. Pole"—I was shameless). I left these drawings all over the room, hoping they would be found during my fictitious trips to the bathroom and office. Once I even scaled off 13 feet along the base of a scale drawing. To my disgust, no one ever picked up my hints—but you may be luckier.

Special Materials:

- Same as Hose Tower (#34), but the point/object must be at the apex of a triangle formed by other objects (ground, phone pole, and guy wire here).

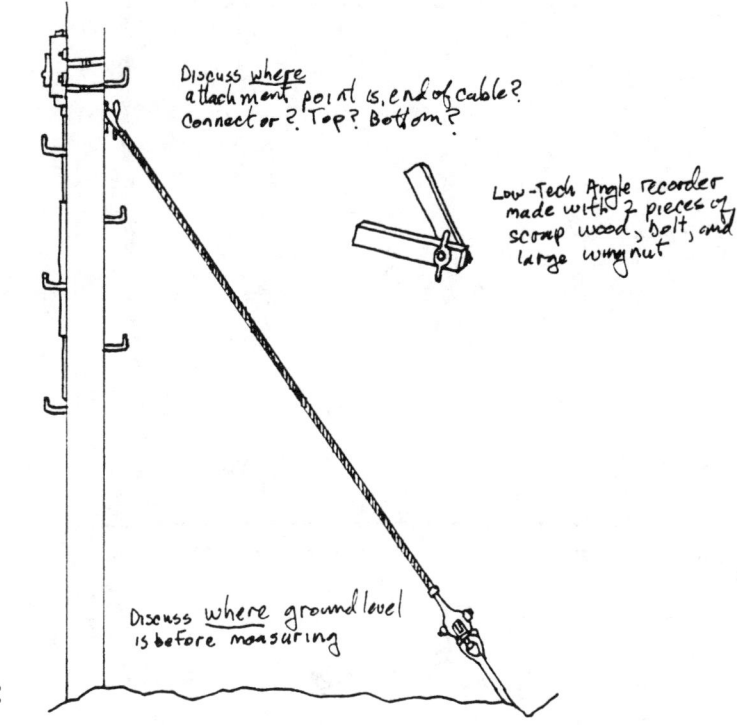

Spinoffs:

1. Ask for the length of the cable.

2. Assign the students with communicating the problem in writing to someone else charged with devising a solution strategy to be communicated over the phone. No drawings allowed.

3. Reverse the procedure outlined for spinoff #2 and require that the students solve the problem for an analogous situation described via letter or the phone for an out-of-sight location. The students must describe a procedure to be used by the on-site person who then carries it out. Again, no drawings.

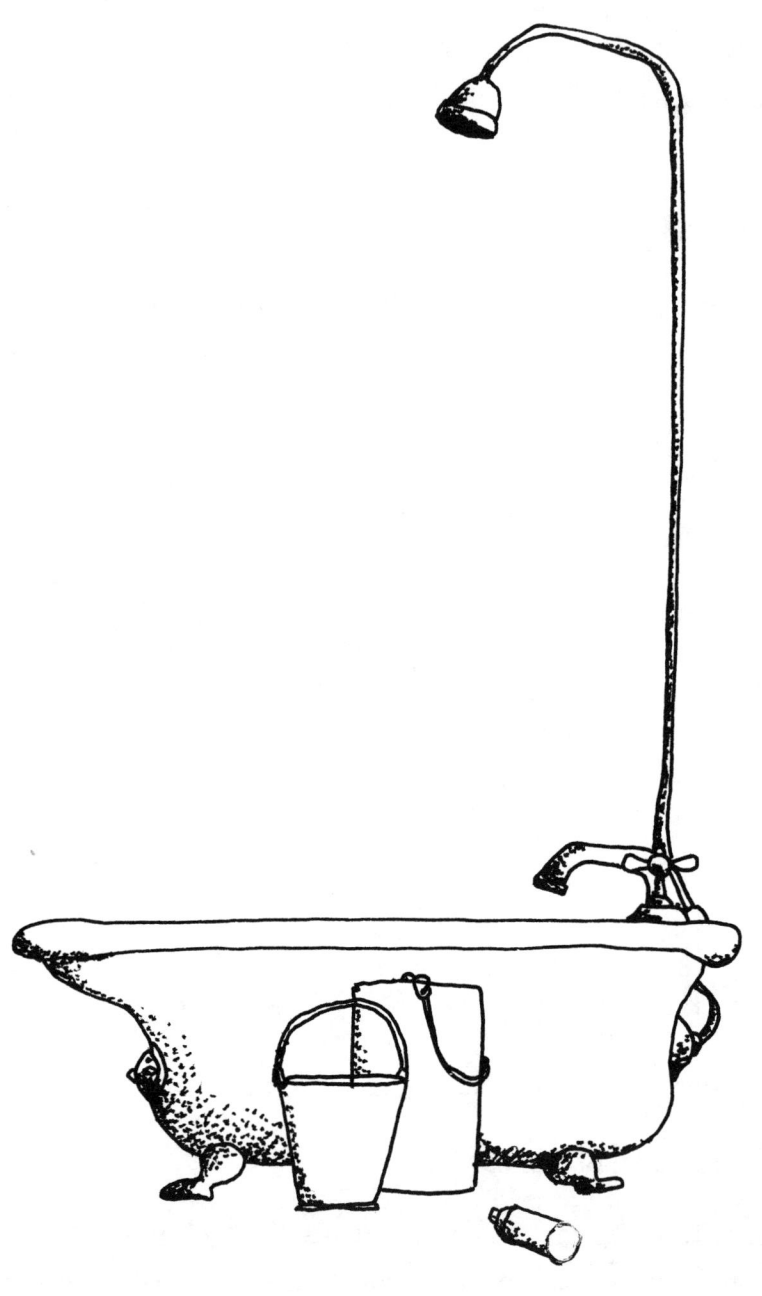

VIII. Flotation and Displacement

Section Notes

These problems are, as a group, the most difficult that I've developed. They are generally messy, time-devouring, and require a lot of preparation—but they're fascinating. They explore Archimedes' idea of displaced water as an indicator of an object's volume, and the relationship of an object's density to its behavior within a surrounding liquid.

A lot of the difficulties arise from the technique we used to measure how much water an object actually does displace. This is something generally left undescribed in textbooks that feature facile statements along the lines of, "an object displaces 1500 ccs. of water. Calculate…" While I understand the theory, I was surprised to find out how difficult it is to actually measure displaced water. Surface tension and the smaller-than-ideal capacities of our triple-beam balances forced us to carefully drip water into containers—an ornery process, given the general level of movement in classrooms even a lot quieter than mine. Once the object is submerged in the quiveringly full container, you must account for water sticking to the bottom of the submerging can when it's lifted out to weigh the spilled water. And simply submerging the object without displacing extra water can be a hard feat in itself, especially if the object is bouyant.

Nevertheless, the floating or sinking of an object is about as pure and dramatic an example as can be conjured up to exemplify the idea of a testable theory or proposition. It's worth the hassles, though many of them might be eliminated by a really accurate graduated cylinder on a larger capacity balance (these would allow measurement of displacement through subtractive methods).

Problem 37 is unusual for this book. Instead of asking whether an object floats, it actually requires a determination of density first—as a concession to the utility of formalizing the relationship between concepts and their practical use at some point.

Problems 38 and 39 are probably the most difficult in the book—work up to them gradually.

36: Don't Cry Over Spilled Milk

Problem: Here are 5 identical coffee cans absolutely filled with water so that *anything* lowered into them will spill water over the sides. *Keep your distance from the table—it took a lot of work to fill these cans just right.* Each can is sitting inside of a larger pan. You get to watch me spill water by dipping each of the 5 objects on the table into its own coffee can of water. Watch carefully; you may need what you see to predict the weights of objects #2 and #4.

Details: Objects #2 and #4 will be locked away in a drawer after their baths. Objects #1, #3, and #5 are yours to fool around with—as long as you don't damage them.

Margin of Error: 4% of the actual weights of objects #2 and #4.

Teacher Notes:

It does take a lot of work to fill them just right—surface tension is an amazing phenomenon. When dipping, attempt to just submerge the entire object. Then lift it carefully from the water and hold it above the surface to get the drips into the can rather than the pan. If you're very conscientious, use tongs (but practice first) or make a wire holder.

I like using two identical regular objects with one of them visibly twice the volume of the other. The third object could be something irregularly shaped or something twice the size of the larger of the first two. What you hope for is that someone notices that each larger object seems to spill about twice the amount spilled by its half-size twin. Wooden blocks and large plastic rods worked well. Use something large enough to displace 50-100 cc.'s of volume.

Originally, I wanted to supply the filled weights of all cans and simply let kids subtract the weight of the missing water to determine how much had been displaced. Unfortunately, a coffee can full of water is far too heavy for my balance. Maybe you'll be more resourceful in locating an industrial-strength balance. If not, after the object is dipped and removed, lift the can and let any water on the sides or bottom drip into the pan before removing the can to a distance from the pan. The procedure is mysterious and provoking.

Special Materials:

- 5 coffee cans filled 1 drop shy of overflowing (this takes patience)

- 5 pans to catch displaced water

- 5 or more objects of 4 to 8 cubic inches volume each. There should be at least 2 made of one material, and all of the objects should be made of materials readily available (wood, plastic, etc.) in easily measured shapes

- Pipettes

- Triple-beam balance—if possible, one will weigh 2,000 grams, so that your students can simply weigh the can after the water has been displaced. Or, locate a very accurate graduated cylinder that allows students to "read" the decrease in volume caused by removing an object from it.

- Tongs or other tool for holding object with minimal added volume

- Paper towels and sponges

Spinoffs:

1. Fill a smaller can with water after a non-floating object is placed in it. Then remove the object and let them work on how much the level drops. Allow object to drip over can before removing it altogether in order to get a truer displacement.

37: Lucite Rod

Problem: Without touching the rod with any water, find its density in grams per cubic centimeter and predict whether or not it will float in water. Explain your reasoning and be ready to bet $10 on your prediction.

Extra: Will it float in mercury? oil? alcohol? How do you know?

Teacher Notes:

This is a pretty text-bookish problem designed to formalize ideas about what is true about an object that floats in a surrounding medium.

Special Materials:

- Round plastic rod, approximately 8" long and 1" diameter
- Another rectangular object made of the same plastic
- Water-filled container large enough to float or sink the rod
- Triple-beam balance

Spinoffs:

1. In which of the listed materials will the rod float most easily?
2. Most people float in the ocean, but only some do in lakes. Have the students speculate on the reason for this difference and then devise a way to test it.

38: Balloons

Problem: Assemble an amount of weight (including a method for attaching it to the balloon) small enough that the balloon won't quite sink to the bottom of the bucket when we put it in—but large enough that when I add two pennies, it will sink.

Details: You're really trying to figure out how much weight the balloon is able to lift in water. Since I'm a nice guy, you may put the balloon in water as often as you like. Since I'm not *that* nice, you may not put anything else in the water with the balloon. When you have an estimate of the proper weight (including the attaching apparatus), secure it to the balloon, and we will hit the water with 2¢ for a test of your Aquatic Prognostication.

Margin of Error: 2 cents

Teacher Notes:

This was a great problem—for me. I found the whole operation beautiful and mysterious, as did about 3 students. The balloon suspended in the still water is really compelling for those of us who still like to play in the bathtub. Its silent sinking at the addition of a single penny was electrifying.

Unfortunately, most of the class found the steps necessary to get to these magical moments both tiresome and difficult to attend. Getting the volume of the balloon through displacement was quite difficult, even for the students who understood the concept well. Balloons are just not easy to carefully submerge into a container absolutely filled with water. There were numerous pan dryings and bucket refillings (it might be worth exploring a close-to-zero-volume attachment that will hold the balloon under water. This would allow measurement of displacement by measurement of the difference between the water level of the bucket when it held the balloon and when it did not).

The problem was, however, very valuable to the few who stuck with it. I think if I were to offer this again, it would be to 3 or 4 students only. This would allow involvement without chaos (the water displacement phase requires care and technique, neither of which is enhanced by large numbers). To spread the benefit, it could be offered as a special project which could then be presented by the small group to the rest of the class. This is not in keeping with orthodox inquiry-based liturgy, but sometimes one has to compromise.

In general, I'd encourage you, even more than in other instances, to try this one yourself. You'll need a tall bucket—the 5-gallon plastic jobs are great. A sturdy kitchen garbage pail will work if you can find one with a wide enough opening (they're all narrowly rectangular). A turkey roaster makes a suitable pan to catch the displaced water.

When collecting this stuff, remember that you want enough capacity to allow some movement of the balloon up and down in the water, but students will need to be able to lift the bucket and pour displaced water from the pan back into it many times. Two pans, a larger container of room-temperature water, a small transfer bucket, a turkey baster, and a lot of paper towels and newspaper are all good things to have around. Washers and wire worked well for the attachment and weight.

Special Materials:

- 5-gallon bucket
- Balloons—one should be inflated to a size (6" to 10") that will allow it to fit between the sides of the bucket
- Wire and washers
- String
- Pennies
- Paper towels and sponges

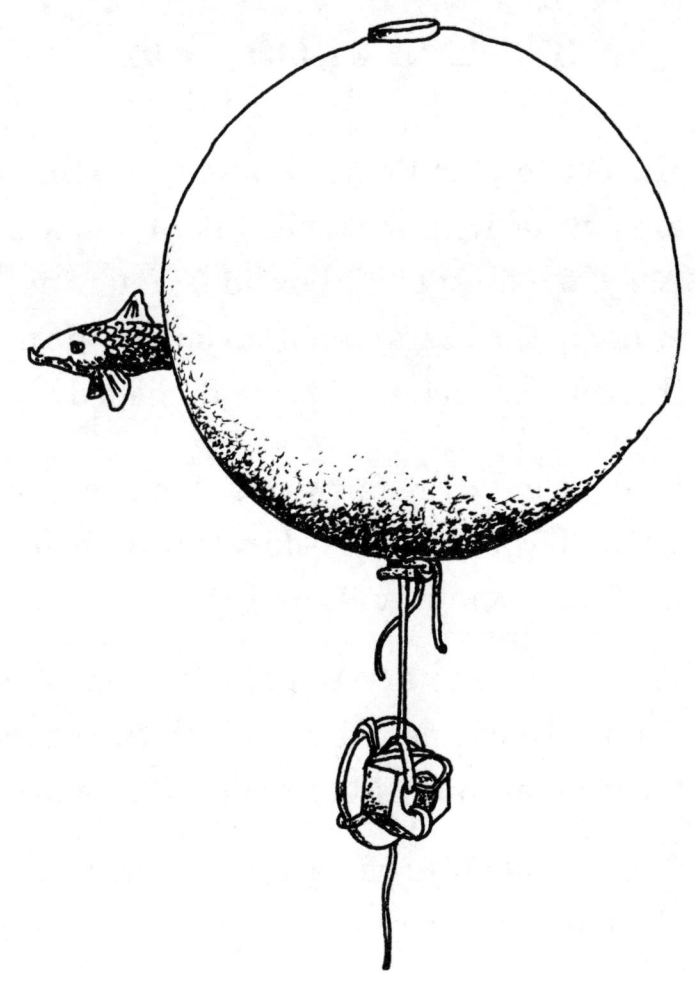

Spinoffs:

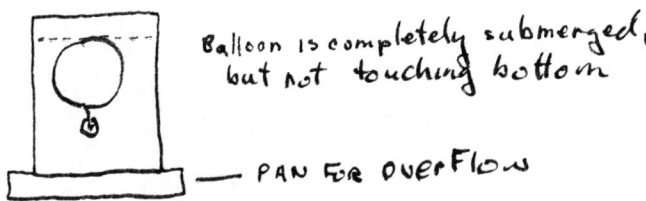

1. What will happen if they re-suspend the balloon and carefully add salt to the water? Have them demonstrate their prediction through another experiment. Then let them try it with the balloon and a box of Morton's.

2. What will happen if ice cubes (lots) are carefully put in the water holding the balloon suspended between the bottom and the surface? (There are actually thermometers based upon this idea.)

38: Balloons

39: End of the Year

Problem: You get to play Boats. You need to find the *minimum* amount of weight it will take to sink boats C and D (they're really plastic box lids). You're not allowed to get either of the boats wet, but you may do anything else to them as long as they aren't damaged.

Details: Boats A and B are fair game. Float 'em, sink 'em, collect 'em with your friends—do whatever helps you figure out the "sink weight" of C and D.

To make this interesting, divide yourselves into 2 even teams and compete to see which team can come up with the *smallest* amount of weight that will sink each boat.

This is probably the hardest problem you've been given all year. Consider it your final exam.

Margin of Error: Your sense of style and confidence in your ability.

Teacher Notes:

Although you might not agree with my assessment of this as the most difficult problem, take my word for it—it's not a good one to start with.

Take some time to find rectangular boats made of the same material. If you use plastic, like I did, make sure it's the same kind and of the same thickness. Try this yourself...you may learn more than you bargained for.

Special Materials:

- 4 rectangular (plastic or other) containers (boats) with open tops and of different sizes
- Buckets or containers large enough to float the boats
- Triple-beam balance
- Washers, Pennies, BB's, etc.

Spinoffs:

1. Ask that the weight be such that the boat will support it but sink with the addition of a single penny.

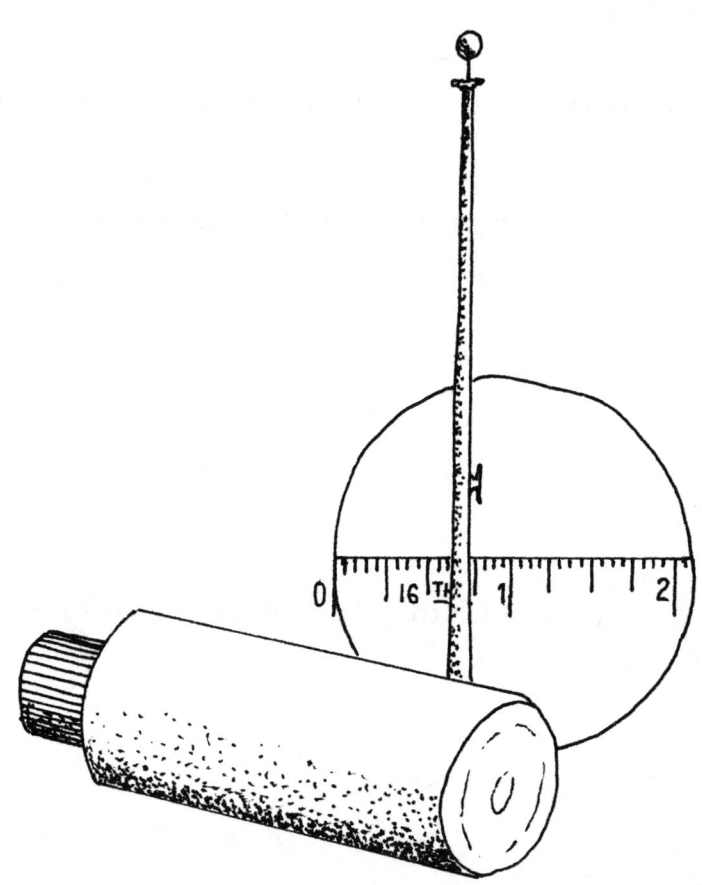

IX. Odds and Ends

Section Notes

Here are problems that were never tried, were underdeveloped, or just didn't seem to fit into any of the other sections. Problems 40, 41, 43, and 44 generally treat issues of scale, comparing the distorted (e.g. shrunken or expanded) image of an object of known size to something (similarly distorted) of unknown size. They generally require walking around town and are good at the end of the year—for those odd moments that seem to abound in June.

Problem 42 is a gold mine for science teachers who want to trust the inquiry-based approach but just can't. It represents the most successful blending I've ever achieved of "covering the material" (in this case, the relationship between temperature and volume of a liquid) but through an inquiry-driven process. The problem was actually developed out of student questions and really produced one of those cartoon idea-lightbulbs over someone's head.

Problem 45 is an odd twist of a volume determination problem that just didn't quite fit elsewhere.

Problem 46 is, depending on the shaker used, a volume problem or a group process/estimation exercise. It can be a great one for getting kids to work together.

Problem 47 probably should have gone into the density/identity section, but I never tried it out due to its "technical difficulties."

The fact that these problems were not tightly integrated into other work is not necessarily an indication of their value or relationship to other concepts explored in other problems. You might weave any of these into other blocks of problems.

40: Looking Down and Out

Problem: Using only the aerial photo and other things in the classroom, find the location and length of the side of the marked parking lot. Then write a set of directions exact enough so that Jim can follow them to the parking lot from the front door of the school. He knows nothing about the area and will literally do only what you tell him. You may not leave the building. We'll follow Jim and check your estimate by measuring the side of the parking lot (hopefully).

Margin of Error:

Teacher Notes: This is fun and worthwhile if you can obtain a good photo (City Planning often has them). The problem hinges on the location of any object of known size. The strategies by which students have done this while in the building have been fascinating (there are actually students who can absolutely identify specific truck and car models from pictures taken at 3,000 feet). Some students discover City Planning, too. Interestingly, in their efforts to "cheat," they have found that the figures provided by municipal offices for many measurements are not exact—an insightful commentary on the value of trusting your own resources rather than those of others who may not require the same degree of accuracy that you do. A 6" to 1' margin of error is about right for this one.

Special Materials:
- Aerial photo of town and/or area around the school
- 50' tape measure

Spinoffs:
1. Blindfold Jim.
2. Estimate the number of bicycle wheel revolutions needed to cover the length of the parking lot.
3. Obtain a picture from another unfamiliar city where you have a cooperative friend. Have the friend check student estimates of size after a student representative calls with instructions.

41: Cuban Missile Base

Problem: Using this aerial photo as evidence, the Albanian Embassy has accused the City of Concord of harboring a Cuban Missile Base and declared that the building marked on the photo houses two fully-deployed Cuban-manned SS-20 missiles—and two spares. Is this possible? Support your conclusion with figures and prepare to answer reporters' questions at a press conference.

Details: Unfortunately, as vitally important defense experts, you may not leave the building and must rely completely on data you can obtain from your safe classroom location: An SS-20 is 37.5 meters long and, when deployed on its launcher, requires a storage area 42.3 m. x 11.6 m.

TOP SECRET U.S.D.O.D. Satellite Recon. Photo B/2·17
AERIAL VIEW - KNARSK (U.S.S.R) SS-20 INSTALLATION

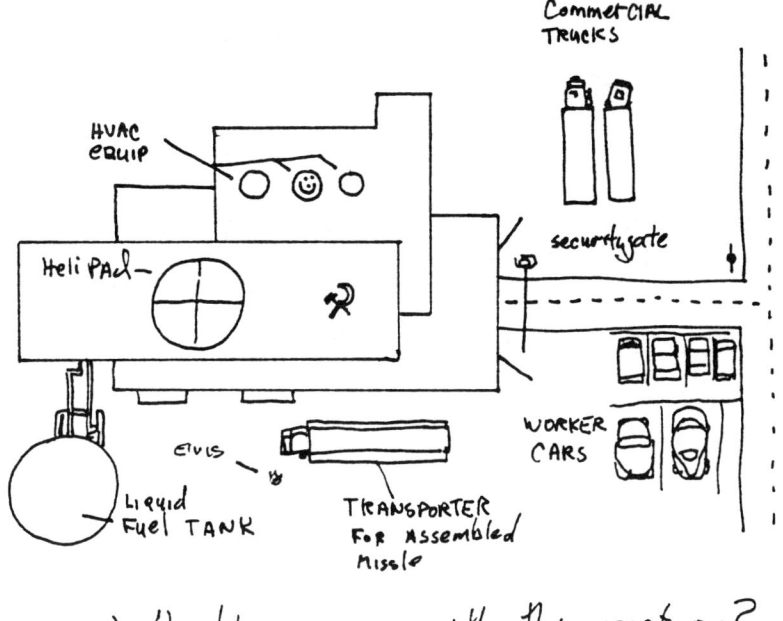

What's wrong with this picture?

Teacher Notes:

You'll need an aerial photo of your town before rewriting this one. Make sure that you cut off the printed scale at the corner. Hopefully, when you attempt this problem, it will seem a little less realistic than it might have been when written (if you remember, the U.S. blockaded Cuba on the basis of this sort of evidence). In any case, the problem's essence can certainly be adapted to other scenarios.

Special Materials:

- Aerial photo of town and/or area around the school. Doctor your photo with official looking marks and dimensions
- 50' tape measure

42: Heavy Water

Problem #1: Does cold water weigh more, less, or the same as hot water? You're given a supply of nearly frozen water, a camping stove, some pipettes, and three 100-ml. volumetric flasks. If you need to heat water, do so in the pan—don't heat the flasks directly.

Problem #2: Tell me the exact temperature of the 100 ml. of water that I'll pour and pipette into one of the flasks. I'll weigh the water and flask before dipping in a thermometer—which you will not be allowed to read. I'll read it and write down the temperature of the water immediately and keep this data in my pocket.

Problem #3: Predict what will happen if I put 100 ml. of water at 70° C. on the balance with the thermometer in it, weigh it, and then leave it on the balance as it cools. Predict what will happen if I do the same thing with 10° C. water and let it warm up. Justify your predictions with reasons.

After you have formed your predictions, divide into groups according to what you expect. I'll then test both operations. If your group is correct, you'll have to explain your reasoning to the other groups. If no group successfully predicts the outcome, you'll all need to rethink the problem until you can come up with a theory that fits the facts.

Teacher Notes:

Few groups can get through this without a lot more explanation—but the effort has been more than worth it. One class spent 3 hours weighing 100-ml. volumes of different temperatures of water, graphing the weights by temperature. That really slammed them into issues of procedure, interpolation, and extrapolation; they learned when to suspect their own results. A lot of good came out of it—and they ended up with a fairly accurate way to predict water temperature by weight.

All of this requires a lot of concern with procedure as the weight changes are very small. Flasks need to be thoroughly dried and reweighed before each reuse. The balance needs to be perfectly zeroed. Also, when the water is warm, there is a problem with removing condensed droplets from the neck of the flask (careful use of pipette and rolled sticks of kleenex worked fairly well.) This is another one you want to try on your own unless you are very confident of being able to switch gears and shift with the terrain as it changes. There are some very frustrating moments built into this one. For my money, though, it was ample justification to watch a group of students think their way out of the apparent contradiction presented by the fact that they "proved" cold water to be heavier than hot, but did not observe any change in the weight of 100 ml. of hot water that was allowed to cool.

Special Materials:

- Two 100-mL volumetric flasks
- Pipettes
- Stove or camping stove
- Ice water
- Lab thermometer on string
- Paper towels and tissues
- Triple-beam balance
- 50' tape measure

43: Fire Hose

Problem: Describe—to another group of students—the fire hose folded on the rack in the hallway.

Details: You must do so without unfolding it or touching it—and without speaking or hand signalling to your audience. If you use paper or a computer, you may show only one number to the other group—and that number must *not* be your estimate of the hose's total length.

Margin of Error: Your description must allow them to determine the hose's length to within 8 inches.

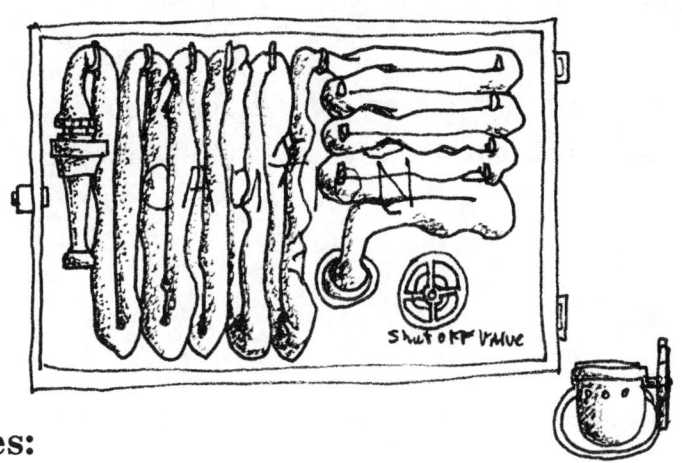

Teacher Notes:

This seemed a great idea, but I never got it off of the ground. I envisioned kids producing fabulous drawings on graph paper. They would explore issues of scale and accuracy. I got complaints that it was a stupid problem. I'm not sure whether it's in the format or the problem itself, but I still think it's worth working on.

Special Materials:

- Fire hose or other object that is convoluted, or irregularly twisted in a two dimensional plane.

44: Rain Gutter

Problem: Without leaving the room, use the photograph of Chuck standing behind the building (or any other information you can obtain without leaving the room) to determine the exact vertical distance between the ground and the bottom of the second-story rain gutter at the point where it passes directly over his head.

Margin of Error: 1 inch

Teacher Notes:

Have your scale person stand on a level board or platform and mark the measuring point so as not to be troubled by where to measure from later.

Special Materials:

- Photo (available to the students) of a person standing by a large building or object.

Spinoffs:

1. Supply the height from ground to gutter and ask for the person's height instead (of course, use someone not available to students.)
2. Have your person slouch or bend at the waist.

45: Puddle

Problem: Without opening it, determine how large a puddle the water inside the sealed tube will make if it's opened and allowed to flow onto the table. Keep in mind that you'll also have prove the size of the puddle if it happens to assume a different shape than you expect.

Margin of Error:

Teacher Notes:

A never-used problem, its intended outcome is a simple transformation of a calculated volume of water into weight. Nevertheless, some other interesting things might be discovered about areas of things that are neither rigid nor flat.

Special Materials:

- 2' to 10' of transparent plastic flexible tubing, one large piece and one small one (6" or less)—with the large piece sealed at both ends by melting them shut with an iron or heated screwdriver blade.
- Pipettes
- Triple-beam balance
- A table that you can soak without getting fired

46: Salt Shaker

Problem: Find out how many grains of salt are in the shaker without opening it or removing any of the salt. No other shakers, please.

Margin of Error:

Teacher Notes:

Find the most simply-shaped salt shaker possible. The fact that other shakers cannot be used makes this a problem of estimation and volume—because the students cannot use weight as an easy volume indicator. Obviously, a good portion of the activity involves counting the salt crystals in a systematic and reliable way.

Special Materials:

- Transparent salt shaker, partially full
- Small amount of salt

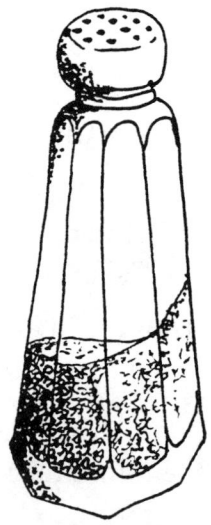

Spinoffs:

1. Have the students look at salt, sugar, and sand under a microscope (or large magnifying glass), then use their observations to predict the number of sand grains and sugar granules needed to fill the shaker to the same point. Have them check the accuracy of their predictions and re-evaluate their theories, if necessary.

47: Heavy

Problem: On the table are two solid objects, supposedly made of iron. Are they made of exactly the same metal? Is either one made from pure iron? Prove your determinations.

Teacher Notes:

This was never tried. I collected the solid bottom of an antique iron and a 1 kg. weight used on a commercial balance, but I didn't have a group ready to tackle a problem of this difficulty. It calls for either a lot of research into possible chemical and/or heat tests (which involve melting, etc.) or a determination of density. If the shapes are complex, water displacement can determine volume—but the weights of my objects both greatly exceeded the capacity of my little lab scales. This called for a student-fabricated balance or my finding a larger-capacity balance.

Also, establishing the true identities of the metals requires metallurgical tests, or the location of a reliably pure piece of iron, or a listing of iron's density. Other materials might have worked equally well, but I wanted one that might occur in a near elemental state so that it would have been possible to compare the object's density to a findable specific gravity (an element.) Aluminum was another good possibility, but I was unable to find solid objects of suitable size. For reasonable accuracy, I needed objects that would displace at least 100 cc's.

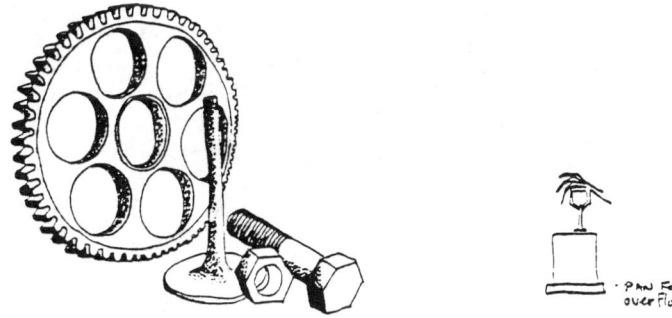

Special Materials:

- Two solid-seeming objects apparently made of the same metal.
- Scale or balance capable of weighing 3,000 grams

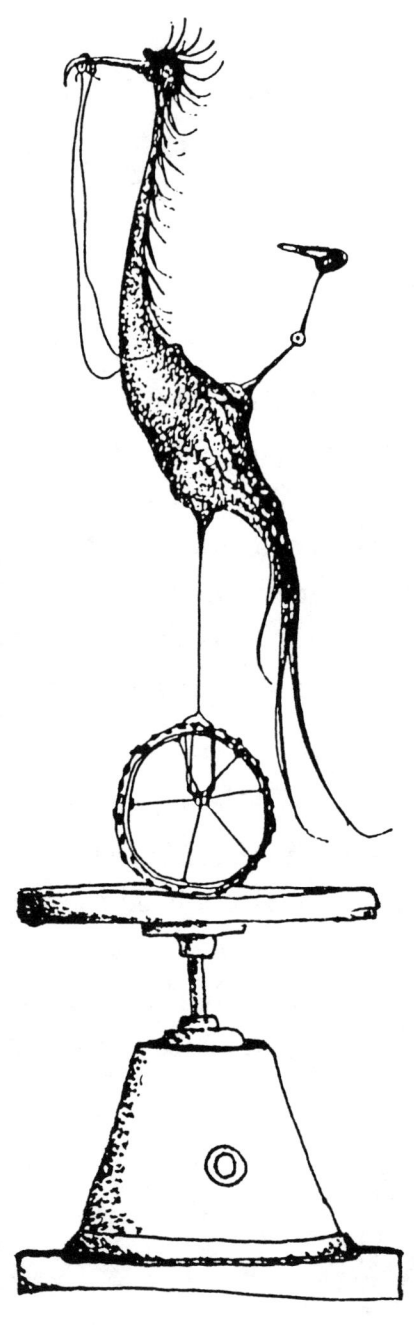

For Future Thought

More Problem-Solving Situations

To contact author/instructor **Joel Greenberg** about your experiences with any of his Problem-Solving Situations in this volume—or to arrange workshops with him for your school or district on this inquiry-based approach—write to Grapevine Publications at the address below.

Hopefully, the problems in this book have helped you—and made you wish for more. Well, as you might have noticed, the title of this book says "Volume 1." Grapevine is now collecting and gathering additional Problem-Solving Situations, for Volume 2. So if you have some P.S.S.'s that you've used in class and would like to contribute to such a volume, send your submittals to:

> **Problem-Solving**
> Grapevine Publications, Inc.
> P.O. Box 2449
> Corvallis, OR 97339-2449

What makes a good Problem-Solving Situation?

1. It demands that the students make a *testable prediction* (and preferably testable by the *students*).

2. It makes use of relatively inexpensive equipment. Fancier equipment might be used (to obtain higher precision), but the problem should work well at the low-tech end of the spectrum.

3. It should be complex enough to elicit multiple problem-solving approaches from the students.

4. It should benefit from (as opposed to being hindered by) group effort.

A Precollege Math/Science Curriculum

Problem-Solving Situations are designed to enrich a traditional math/science curriculum. Depending upon how they're used, the situations could be used effectively in an upper elementary, middle school, junior high school, or high school setting. They are designed to give students experience handling the pressures of real problem-solving and making scientific predictions—before they even attempt the more complex experimentation of high school biology and chemistry.

However, the *Problem-Solving Situations* series is not intended to be a curriculum by itself. Rather, it is a preparation for a robust high school math/science curriculum. One example of such a curriculum is Grapevine's *Doing Science Project*.

The *Doing Science Project* is being built around interactive learning, and so it leans heavily on the inquiry and problem-solving approach—as modeled here in *Problem-Solving Situations*. It makes consistent use of small groups working on concrete real-world projects. It uses multiple sources of information—reference books, journal articles, computer databases, experimental data, etc. Students learn to take responsibility for the learning they do. Teachers don't "Know the Answers;" instead they act as experienced guides to getting the answers.

Already such an approach is being tested in classrooms for interactive college prep mathematics (grades 9-11): *The Interactive Math Project*, developed by the EQUALS program at the Lawrence Hall of Science at Berkeley is an excellent example of the interactive learning principles espoused here, and it promises to be a very effective curriculum over a wide range of student abilities.*

Therefore Grapevine's *Doing Science Project* is now being developed as a similar curriculum in college prep science. This curriculum "covers" all of the conceptual and behavioral objectives now required for college entrance—but not in the traditional lock-step. Instead of teaching concepts of biology one year, those of chemistry in another, and the requisite math in another class altogether, interactive learning is inherently integrated.

* For more information about the *Interactive Math Project*, contact Sherry Fraser, EQUALS, Lawrence Hall of Science, University of California, Berkeley CA 94720 (415) 642-1823.

Furthermore, the laboratory component of *Doing Science* is not an adjunct to the conceptual curriculum; it is seamlessly built into it. The lab experiments in the interactive curriculum have a real sense of discovery about them—as they should. After all, science is the process of posing questions and looking for verifiable answers about the real world—answers that one can't "look up in the book."

If you would like to be involved in the development process of the *Doing Science Project*, you can receive more information by writing to:

The Doing Science Project
Grapevine Publications, Inc.
P.O. Box 2449
Corvallis, OR   97339-2449

We have many other great books for learning about your computer and your favorite software—don't miss them!

An Easy Course in Using DOS

Here's the fastest, easiest way to get up-to-speed on DOS—the heart of your IBM or IBM-compatible personal computer! **An Easy Course in Using DOS** is a clear, "plain-English" course in all facets of the powerful DOS operating system, with the example-rich, conversational format and humor that Grapevine has become so well-known for. This Easy Course even gives a short history of the development of computers and operating systems, too!

An Easy Course in Using Lotus 1-2-3

Here's the fastest, easiest way to get up-to-speed on Lotus 1-2-3! This book applies to **Release 2.2** and any earlier versions of Lotus, giving you practical, hands-on lessons in the basics of **spreadsheets**, **databases**, and **graphs**.

Each lesson shows you working examples of the commands you need to learn—and as you progress through the lessons, you'll be building and modifying your own working spreadsheet.

We have Easy Courses and related books on many other subjects. Contact us for a free catalog!

Grapevine Publications, Inc.
P.O. Box 2449
Corvallis, OR 97339-2449
1-800-338-4331

Reader Comments

We here at Grapevine love to hear feedback about our publications. It helps us produce books tailored to our readers' needs. If you have any specific comments or advice for our authors after reading this book, we'd appreciate hearing from you!

Which of our books do you have?

Comments, Advice and Suggestions:

May we use your comments as testimonials?

Your Name: Profession:
City, State:

Please send Grapevine Catalogues to the following persons:

Name _____
Address _____
City _____ State _____ Zip _____

Name _____
Address _____
City _____ State _____ Zip _____

To Order **Grapevine Publications** books:

- ☏ **Call** to charge the books to **VISA/MasterCard**, *or*
- ✍ **Send** this Order Form to: **Grapevine Publications, P.O. Box 2449 Corvallis, OR 97339**

Qty.	Item #	Book Title	Unit Cost	Total

Shipping Information:

Post Office shipping and handling .... ADD $ 2.50
    (allow 2-3 weeks for delivery).............................. *or*
UPS shipping and handling .... $.75
    (allow 7-10 days for delivery) .... *or*
International Book Surface Post .... $ 4.50
    (allow 6-8 weeks for delivery)
<u>Air Parcel</u> (Please contact us for the correct amount or add $10 per book to Canada and Mexico. Add $25 per book to all other countries. We will refund any cash excess, or charge exact shipping cost to credit cards. Allow 2-3 weeks for delivery)

Subtotal	
Shipping See shipping Info.	
TOTAL	

Payment Information

☐ **Check** enclosed (Please **make your check** payable to **Grapevine Publications, Inc.**)
    (International Check or Money Order must be in U.S. funds and drawn on a U.S. bank)

☐ **VISA** or **MasterCard #** _____ Exp. date _____

Your Signature _____

Name_____ Phone (____) _____

Shipping Address_____
    (Note: UPS will not deliver to a P.O. Box! Please give a street address for UPS delivery)
City_____ State _____ Zip _____ Country_____